Romanticism
and the
Androgynous Sublime

Romanticism
and the
Androgynous Sublime

Warren Stevenson

Madison • Teaneck
Fairleigh Dickinson University Press
London: Associated University Presses

Associated University Presses
440 Forsgate Drive
Cranbury, NJ 08512

Associated University Presses
16 Barter Street
London WC1A 2AH, England

Associated University Presses
P.O. Box 338, Port Credit
Mississauga, Ontario
Canada L5G 4L8

The paper used in this publication meets the requirements
of the American National Standard for Permanence of Paper
for Printed Library Materials Z39.48-1984.

Library of Congress Cataloging-in-Publication Data

Stevenson, Warren.
    Romanticism and the androgynous sublime / Warren Stevenson.
      p. cm.
    Includes bibliographical references and index.
    ISBN 0-8386-3668-3 (alk. paper)
    1. English poetry—19th century—History and criticism.
2. Androgyny (Psychology) in literature.   3. Sublime, The, in
literature.   4. Romanticism—England.   5. Femininity (Psychology) in
literature.   6. English poetry—Men authors—History and criticism.
I. Title.
PR545.A49S74   1996
821'.709353—dc20

               95-43311
               CIP

For M.

"Human nature was originally one and we were a whole, and the desire and pursuit of the whole is called love."

—Plato, *Symposium,* trans. B. Jowett

"The Sublime is the image of a great soul."

—Longinus, *On the Sublime*

"The truth is, a great mind must be androgynous."

—Samuel Taylor Coleridge, *Table-Talk*

Contents

Preface

To LEVEL WITH THE READER—ALWAYS A DANGEROUS UNDERTAK-ing in these deciduous and neotheoretical days: it is my considered conviction that what we as individuals call *sublime,* insofar as we use the word at all, is now virtually indistinguishable from what we consider to be first-rate poetry or art. "My favorite poet (or critic) is sublime; yours produces beautiful verse (or criticism); his writes terrible stuff," would be a caricature of the prevailing situation, but only a slight one. Couched in the current argot, the sublime is, or has tended to become, "whatever turns you on."

This of course is not what the romantics meant by the term. What they did mean seems to have been twofold: either that which lifts you up, out of yourself, to the highest imaginative level, or (more subtly) that which rarefies (not *reifies*) you and either the text you happen to be reading or the landscape you are beholding. Such an experience was—all too briefly, I now realize—mine upon climbing the Lauberhorn (Byron's "*Wengren* [sic] Alp") with two other members of the Byron Society in the summer of 1990.* This impromptu experience turned out to be not only quite unexpected but also different in kind from what, misled by certain eighteenth-century theorists and some of the less memorable effusions of the romantics, I had tended to associate with such strenuous enter-prises. Far from any sense of egotistical aggrandisement, there was rather (somehow enhanced by the physical exhaustion resulting from the relatively brief but hectic ascent), an almost delayed-action sense of déjà vu. Time stopped, at least momentarily, and one felt one had seen those panoramic vistas before, or was always meant to see them *now,* in such a way that they became truly *meta*-physical, involving "[n]o *conscious* memory of a kindred sight" (Wordsworth, *Prelude,* 1.574, my emphasis).

---

*Of our sextet of hardy Byronists who began the scramble to the peak, the two others who completed it (in the same time recorded by Hobhouse for himself and Byron—fifty minutes) were Mr. Michael Rees, who reached the summit first and whose idea it was, and Professor Itsuyo Higashinaka. For further details see *The Byron Journal* (1991) 193, and see ch. 2, "Wordsworth . . . ," n. 11.

What this had to do with androgyny I didn't then know, but have since come to realize that, like sublimity, psychic androgyny—the only kind worth writing about—is itself metaphysical, a transcendence of self and sex in a moment (Blake's "Eternal Now") of total otherness *and* integration. It is a condition to which we can wittingly (as well as unwittingly) aspire, with the growing awareness that in such moments as those offered by both imaginative and linguistic resources we are not only greater than we know, but also, as the romantics so rightly intimated, one with that greatness.

Acknowledgments

I WOULD LIKE TO THANK MICHAEL BULLOCK, JACK STEWART, KAY Stockholder, and Irene Dehnel, each of whom read parts of this book, and Lorne Macdonald, who read the entire manuscript. Their suggestions were invaluable, though the errors are of course my own. Thanks to others who helped in a variety of ways, sometimes least expected. A special thanks to my students, who have provoked, encouraged, amazed, and often anticipated me.

W. S.

Introduction

THIS BOOK HAS A TWOFOLD ORIGIN: IT IS PARTLY AN OUTGROWTH of my long-standing interest in the creation motif and, more recently, the motif of the double in English romantic literature, and partly a sequel to my *Poetic Friends,* a study of literary relations among romantic poets, of which a woman of my acquaintance, herself a poet, remarked: "Where are the women [writers in your book]?" Far from setting out deliberately to rectify this imbalance—apart from critics, who are legion, there are few "women," as such, in this book either, primarily for historical reasons—I found the theme of the present work forcing itself on me when I was trying to write a more conventional study of the mode of the sublime in English romantic poetry, on which a certain amount of work has, fortunately, already been done. I am particularly indebted to Thomas Weiskel, whose book *The Romantic Sublime* I have read not without wonder and delight, while also being provoked into carrying the idea a stage further—something that Weiskel himself seems to invite. Indeed, perhaps this book requires a sequel (written by someone more qualified than I) on the motif of androgynous sublimity as manifested by women writers of the period.[1]

Northrop Frye has remarked somewhere that no literary critic of any experience will take much trouble to define his or her terms; and although the name most intimately associated with the sublime in literary history is that of Longinus, the first-century Greek author of what is still the best treatise on the subject, a mid-eighteenth-century critic complained that "*Longinus* has *entirely* passed over the Inquiry of what the *Sublime* is." This persistent sort of complaint is hardly fair to Longinus: sublimity is as difficult to define as poetry, and for similar reasons.[2] In Neil Hertz's aptly titled *The End of the Line,* the author observes that Longinus takes seriously Socrates' view (as expressed in the Phaedrus) that an ideal discourse is like a living creature, with its own body, as it were, and Hertz cites Longinus's commentary on one of Sappho's most passionate odes as an example of this, although he does not discuss androgyny per se. And so it goes.[3]

13

Immanuel Kant had no direct impact on British romantic poetry, but his continuing influence on aesthetic theory makes some reference to his *Critique of Aesthetic Judgement* useful in a work of this sort. In spite of Kant's idealism, his somewhat obsessive distinctions between subject and object, and the sublime and the beautiful, make him come down for the most part on the anti-androgynous side of the psychic equation. As Blake and Byron, for instance, were aware, the sublime *contains* the beautiful even while transcending it: see p. 45 and Note 36 and p. 88. Unlike Longinus, Kant eschews poetic examples, with the result that his discourse tends to be abstract and apoetical.

For a different view of Kant see Frances Ferguson, *Solitude and the Sublime: Romanticism and the Aesthetics of Individuation* (London: Routledge, 1992).

Edmund Burke, who anticipated Kant by distinguishing between the sublime and the beautiful, thus bifurcating the aesthetic if not the androgynous egg, refused to discuss Longinus. Blake (who also slights Longinus) said he read Burke with "Contempt & Abhorrence" because he "mock[s] Inspiration & Vision," though the late Vincent Arthur de Luca has shown that "Blake's well-known quarrel with Burke . . . is also an internal debate, enacted within the arena of the poet's own works." De Luca also glances at James Beattie's "quirky derivation of sublime from super lima, 'above the slime or mud of this world' [*Dissertations, Moral and Critical* (London, 1783)],"[4] an idea that, as we shall see, Byron cunningly inverts in his famous apostrophe to Ocean.

In view of this sublime disagreement, it is perhaps necessary to go back to the earliest example of the use of the sublime in connection with style, listed in the *OED:* "Sublime, the highest and statliest manner [of writing], and loftiest deliverance of any that may be" (A. Day's *English Sectorie,* 1586). The etymology of the word is hopelessly tangled: *sub* may mean either "under" or "up from underneath," and the various derivations of *limen,* which may mean either "threshold" or "lintel," are similarly diverse. Small wonder that poststructuralists discussing the word have sometimes not concerned themselves with whose oxymoron was being gored. *Sublimation* has been appropriated by psychologists, and *subliminal* by advertising jargon, where the word has taken on the connotation of something that sneaks up on you from below, like the Morlocks in H. G. Wells's *The Time Machine.* But the way up and the way down, as Heracleitus reminds us, are one and the same; and the semantic ambivalence of the sublime may prove useful in our present study of its relation to the mode and motif of androgyny, with which I suggest it is much more intimately connected than has hitherto been generally supposed.

The myth of the androgyne goes back into prehistory and is found in one form or another in most primitive societies. Its first important appearance in Western philosophy is in Plato's *Symposium* (c. 385 B.C.), in his dialogue on the origin and nature of love. After several other attempts have been made to solve the mystery, Aristophanes comes forward with his own explanation:

> The original human nature was not like the present, but different. The sexes were not two as they are now, but originally, three in number; there was man, woman, and the union of the two, having a name corresponding to this double nature, which had once a real existence, but is now lost, and the word "Androgynous" is only preserved as a term of reproach.[5]

Each of these three types of being, Aristophanes playfully assures his audience, was spherical and moved by rolling; but each had a different origin. The males were descended from the sun, the females from the earth, and the bisexual billiard balls (as we may well call the last group) from the moon, alleged to contain both sun and earth. Proud of their wholeness, these ovoid creatures challenged the gods, who responded by splitting each sphere in two. Thus divided, each half was condemned to a life spent in search for its missing other.

It is worth noting that in only one out of three of these "split billiard balls"—the original androgynes—would the missing halves be of the opposite sex. Thus Aristophanes' droll story has a built-in heterophobic bias, which clearly emerges in the following passage: "Men who are a section of that double nature which was once called Androgynous are lovers of women; adulterers are generally of this breed, and also adulterous women who lust after men." By the same token, this curiously seminal myth also asserts that original wholeness *may* be either homosexual or heterosexual.[6] This is a point to which Shelley, who had translated the *Symposium,* adverts towards the end of *Adonais* when he exclaims apropos of his longing to join Keats in the eternal world, "No more let Life divide what Death can join together" (477). Doubtless there is also a connection between Plato's myth of egg-shaped androgynes and Pelasgian as well as Hindu creation myths involving the splitting of a primordial Universal Egg, whose divided parts became heaven and earth.[7]

The androgynous ideal, as Norman O. Brown has shown, comes up in Freud's *Beyond the Pleasure Principle* and Jung's concept of the collective unconscious, and has also been persistently kept alive in both Jewish and Christian mystical traditions:

> In the West, cabalistic mysticism has interpreted Genesis 1:27—"God Created man in his own image . . . male and female created he them"— as implying the androgynous nature of God and of human perfection before the Fall. [I.e., if God made humans in his own image, and there is only one God, then that makes God an androgyne.] From cabalism this notion passed into the Christian mysticism of Boehme, where it is fused with the Pauline mysticism of Galatians 3:28—"There can be no male and female; for ye are all one man in Christ Jesus." . . . [A]s Berdyaev writes: "The great anthropological myth . . . is the myth about the androgyne. . . . Original sin is connected in the first instance with division into sexes and the Fall of the androgyne, i.e., of man as a complete being."[8]

Brown and Berdyaev, like many avant-garde writers before them, are both borrowing from Jacob Boehme, whose first principle, called the *Ungrund* or Abyss, was androgynous, "a masculine virgin, neither woman nor man." Boehme similarly endows God, who arises from the Abyss, with a coeternal feminine counterpart called the Virgin Sophia ("Divine Wisdom"), mentioned in the Book of Proverbs. So too, Boehme not illogically maintained that Adam was dual sexed before God extracted Eve from his rib cage. This idea seems to have fascinated both Jewish rabbis and early German romantic poets.[9]

The idea developed rather differently in England, owing mainly to the influence of Milton, whose portrayal of the Holy Spirit in the opening lines of *Paradise Lost* is androgynous:

> . . . thou from the first
> Wast present, and, with mighty wings outspread
> Dove-like satst brooding on the vast abyss
> And mad'st it pregnant . . .
>
> (1.19–22)

In this passage, which fascinated the English romantic poets, the Holy Spirit becomes both a female dove brooding on the abyss and a male dove impregnating the latter—which is also seen as an aspect of the former. Milton may have had Boehme's androgynous Abyss in mind,[10] but he also seems to have been thinking of the following passage from Psalms: "He shall cover thee with his feathers, and under his wings shalt thou trust" (Ps. 91:4). Here we have a maternal image of God as a mother hen protecting her chicks—

an image adapted by Jesus: "O Jerusalem, Jerusalem . . . how often would I have gathered thy children together, even as a hen gathered her chickens under her wings" (Mat. 23:37). In so far as God has what we call both male and female characteristics, he becomes an androgynous God. This idea too influenced the English romantics.

In his aforementioned book Thomas Weiskel, using Freudian psychology as a convenient metaphor for ontology—in other words, a central myth of our time—sees Coleridge's "Kubla Khan" as portraying what he calls a "phallic hero" emanating from Collins's "rich-haired youth of morn" in his "Ode on the Poetical Character," that is, as a displaced form of sun-worship. While my own approach to "Kubla Khan," fully elaborated elsewhere, tends to be symbolic and archetypal rather than psychological—the only *overt* connection between the sun and the phallus is the fact that some men wake up in the morning with erections—I adduce Weiskel's succinct summary of what other critics, beginning with Frye in *Fearful Symmetry,* have come to recognize as an important romantic archetype:

> The idealized image of the type is the figure of the virile poet identified with the sun and with Phoebus: in Collins, the "rich-haired youth of morn"; in Gray, the aged Bard whose "beard and hoary hair / Streamed like a meteor, to the trouble air"; . . . in the mature Blake, the character Orc subsuming the traditional imagery of the phallic fire. Coleridge celebrated the type—"Beware! Beware! / His flashing eyes, his floating hair"—and Wallace Stevens evokes him splendidly in his "figure of capable imagination . . . a rider intent on the sun, / A youth, a lover with phosphorescent hair, / Dressed poorly, arrogant of his streaming forces."

Weiskel adds a pointed reminder that there is "a darker alternative to the phallic hero," and that "the figure is already demonic; Satan, after all, is his grandfather, the supreme type of the flaming youth who [like Chatterton, according to Wordsworth] perished in his pride."[11] Unmentioned here is the important point that the romantics revalued Milton's portrayal of Satan: for instance, Wallace Stevens's capable rider, at the end of the poem Weiskel refers to,

> . . . created in his mind
> Eventual victor, out of martyrs' bones,
> The ultimate elegance: the imagined land.[12]

The "imagined land" is of course nothing less than Blake's Golgonooza, the Golden Age restored.

Weiskel sees Collins's ode as a subtle, prophetic critique of a certain type of romanticism. "The protagonist of the romance is the rich-haired youth who in Coleridge's phrase, hath drunk the milk of paradise. Daemonic romanticism may be said to commence with the corruption of this youth."[13] One may think of Wordsworth's French mistress, Coleridge's opium addiction, Byron's and Shelley's alienation, and so forth. Where Weiskel goes wrong is in implicitly accepting Collins's fatal (for him) moralism: all six of the major English romantics not only admired Milton, whom they regarded as having more or less successfully combined revolutionary politics with sublime poetics, but also paid him the compliment of imitation, at least during their most productive years.

Here my concern is to follow Weiskel's path—or rather, a path parallel to his—and try to extend it a little further into the forest, bearing in mind Keats's perception that "on the shores of darkness there is light." Following his Freudian path, Weiskel cryptically isolates the dilemma that Collins had prophesied and that each of the romantics faced: "Ultimately the path of the negative or transcendent sublime leads through the phase of daemonic romance, with its oedipal anxieties, to a symbolic identification with the father."[14] Some of the implications of this are worked out in Weiskel's last chapter, "Wordsworth and the Defile of the Word," after which his important study abruptly breaks off for reasons adverted to in the preface, and also, from a different angle, in my chapter on Wordsworth (as ballast) in the present study.

The "way out" that Weiskel seems almost to despair of finding is, I think, to be found in the concept of the androgynous sublime, apprehended as something welling up from below. This is seen in perhaps its purest form in Blake's "To Spring," which continues both stylistically and thematically where Collins leaves off. Whereas Collins's "Ode to Evening" suggests closure, Blake's "To Spring" announces *ouverture*. True, the angelic and (as will be shown), androgynous bridegroom figure descends from above, but the only *sounds* mentioned in the poem—and by implication the poem itself—come from below: "our western isle . . . in full choir hails thy approach, O Spring! / The hills tell each other, and the list'ning / Vallies hear" (3–6). The style is flexuous, limber, expectant.

A similar mode, *mutatis mutandis,* is encountered in Coleridge's "Christabel," Shelley's "The Witch of Atlas," Byron's *Don Juan,* and elsewhere throughout English romantic poetry. The poet *qua* poet is androgynous, which is presumably one of the things Wordsworth meant when he said the poet "has a more comprehensive soul"[15] than is common among humankind. While ascending the Brocken in 1799 Coleridge remarked to Clement Carlyon that the sublime consists in a "suspension of the power of comparison." Thirty-three years later, with unflagging perception, he observed that "a great mind must be androgynous."[16] When due allowance is made for the somewhat sexist terminology of the period, if Blake was right in asserting that "[t]he Poetic Genius is the true Man" and "the body or outward form of Man is derived from the Poetic Genius" (*E*, 2), it follows that we are all imaginatively androgynous, and hence capable of sublimity. It is the contention of the present study that this theme constitutes an important subtext in the poetry of the English romantics.

Romanticism
and the
Androgynous Sublime

1

Blake's Myth of Divine Androgyny

Morninglight: From Androgyny to Philogyny

"To Spring," the first poem in blake's earliest volume, *Poetical Sketches* (1783), is a remarkable lyric that contains the seed of his life's work. In addition to the daring abandonment of rhyme (daring in a lyric: the only previous example that comes readily to mind is Collins's "Ode to Evening") one notices that, far from being a mere abstract personification, Spring is a fully humanized figure, whether male, female, or androgynous.

Usually interpreted as the bridegroom from the Song of Solomon,[1] Spring has "dewy locks," "angel eyes," "holy feet"—a self-reflexive punning reference to the poem's daring prosody?—"perfumed garments," "fair fingers," and bestows "soft kisses" as well as scattering seminal "pearls" on the "love-sick land." That the land is indisputably feminine is indicated by the use of the pronoun "her" (13). But there is no corresponding masculine pronoun used with reference to Spring, and the tantalizing multiple hints of Spring's androgynous nature remain to be interpreted.

My guess is that Blake is indeed adumbrating his later myth, specifically that part of it referred to in the untitled poem prefaced to chapter 4 of *Jerusalem,* written some forty years later:

> England! awake! awake! awake!
>   Jerusalem thy Sister calls!
> Why wilt thou sleep the sleep of death
>   And close her from thy ancient walls.
>
> Thy hills & valleys felt her feet,
>   Gently upon their bosoms move:
> Thy gates beheld sweet Zions ways;
>   Then was a time of joy and love.
>
> And now the time returns again:
>   Our soul exult & Londons towers

23

Recieve the Lamb of God to dwell
In Englands green & pleasant bowers.

(*E*, 231)

Although three rhymed quatrains have replaced four unrhymed
ones, the underlying similarity of imagery and thought remains.
Here the awakener is undeniably feminine, and although Jerusalem
is the emanation of the giant Albion—who is also being called
upon to awaken, and is portrayed embracing her, and by symbolic
extension England, in the illustration to plate 99—the emphasis in
this late lyric may perhaps best be described as transcendentally
homoerotic. So too, it would seem, in "To Spring," where Blake
lays down the guidelines for his evolving myth.

Blake's interest in androgyny is reflected throughout *Poetical
Sketches:* for instance, in the delightful song "Love and harmony
combine," where he avoids specifying the sex of either the speaker
or the beloved who is spoken to, whether animal, vegetable, or
both. In the fourth stanza the turtle dove who "feeds her young"
turns out to be feminine, but her mate is both tantalizingly absent—
"Sweet I hear her *mournful* song" (14; emphasis added)—and present: "There is love: I hear his tongue" (16-17).

In the superb "How sweet I roam'd," said to have been written
by Blake around the age of puberty, the "prince of love" is masculine, but the sex of the speaker is again left deliberately indetermi-
nate, and—lest one should hasten to shout "Blake!"—there are
more intimations of androgyny: "He [the prince of love] shew'd
me lilies for my hair, / And blushing roses for my brow" (5-6).
Blake seems to be saying that from a *poetical* point of view the
sex of the speaker doesn't particularly matter. One is reminded of
John Donne's "Holy Sonnett XIV," wherein the soul of the mystic
is portrayed as feminine in its relation to God, of whom Blake's
Apollonian prince of love may be regarded as a fair enough
surrogate.

Thus the most successful of the *Poetical Sketches* are the ones
in which the speaker, if not the main characters, is portrayed,
directly or indirectly, as androgynous. The perfunctory references
in two of the less memorable songs by a lovesick, presumably
male, speaker to his "black eyed maid" merely tend to confirm
this impression. It is also worth noting that the most memorable
character in "An Imitation of Spenser"—a poem not notable for
its sublimity, but of technical interest—is the "warrior maid invin-
cible, / Arm'd with terrors of Almighty Jove!" (44–45), whose pity
the speaker implores. In Blake's early, unpublished satire "An Is-

land in the Moon," Steelyard the Lawgiver observes *en passant* that women are stronger than men because "A girl always has more tongue than a boy" (*E,* 447).

Tiriel, a re-working of the Oedipus myth with overtones that point in the direction of George III, who was already showing signs of madness when the poem was written (c. 1788), portrays a blind, tragic tyrant seeking vainly to return eastward to the infantile security of a false paradise in the vales of Har, whose only guiding light, à la Sophocles, turns out to be his surviving daughter, Hela. The eyeball-to-eyeball quasi-sexual confrontation of "Har and Heva bathing" portrayed in one of the drawings to this work, which Blake left unpublished, may be a hit at Donne's "The Ecstasy."[2]

In marked contrast to the delicate androgyny of *Poetical Sketches* and the false androgyny of *Tiriel,* differences of gender are clearly delineated throughout *Songs of Innocence,* published by a wonderful irony in the year the French Revolution began. The child who instructs the Piper in the "Introduction" is definitely masculine, and Lyca of "The Little Girl Lost" and "The Little Girl Found" is just as persistently and unforgettably feminine. That Blake eventually transposed these latter two poems to *Songs of Experience* (1794) suggests that Lyca—the name crops up in an early version of "Laughing Song"—is a crucial character, a sort of Blakean Eve who leads the way out of his prelapsarian state into, and ultimately beyond, his postlapsarian one. As in Milton's paradise, the feminine principle is the more dynamic one, the putative masculinity of the creator of the Tyger notwithstanding.

The first critic of this most famous of Blake's short poems, Benjamin Heath Malkin, saw "The Tyger" as in effect an example of the Longinian sublime: "[The poem] rises with its subject. It wears that garb of grandeur which the idea of creation communicates to a mind of a high order."[3] (Longinus had praised the sublimity of the biblical account of the creation in Genesis.) From a modern perspective this observation seems not so much invalid as incomplete. "The Tyger" can now be seen, and is probably apprehended by most readers, consciously or unconsciously, as having a parodic aspect, reinforced by the poem's unexpectedly comic illustration. The text of "The Tyger," except for the fifth stanza, reads almost like a parody of Burke's terrible sublime, which we know Blake abhorred.[4] In terms of Blake's later myth, the Tyger's framer, in more ways than one, is Los while under the domination of his Spectre—that is, while separated from his feminine principle, or emanation.[5]

The all-important exception is the penultimate stanza beginning

"When the stars threw down their spears / And water'd heaven with their tears," wherein the tone changes from one of fury and vengeance to one of compassion and loving-kindness, by implication, at least, involving what may be termed the feminine aspect of God: "Did he smile his work to see? / Did he who made the Lamb make thee?" The metrical and rhetorical emphasis of these crucial lines falls upon the words "smile" and "Lamb," and the stanza as a whole asks the ultimate ontological question in such a way as to evoke from the reader the only truly human image of God in the poem, which would otherwise degenerate into mere rhetorical bluster. Indeed the word *lamb,* when used not as a noun but a verb, is itself androgynous, meaning both to give birth (cf. "made the Lamb") and to shepherd (ewes) at lambing-time *(OED).*

Proleptically, Los is reunited with Enitharmon. This theme is further elaborated in the prophetic books. For instance, in *The Book of Los* there is a similar development when Los "smild with joy" (4.45) upon beholding his creation of the sun—a scene that Blake illustrates in his companion work, *The Song of Los* (pl. 8) where Los's smile, like that on the face of the Tyger, is so deliberately low-keyed that some readers have missed it. "The Tyger" also, of course, has a sociosexual aspect, which, as I have discussed it elsewhere, I do not propose to go into here, except to add that Lyca found "tygers" attractive playmates both during and after her peregrinations.[6] Similarly, at the conclusion of "The Tyger" the foolish questioner, by persisting in his folly and becoming united with his androgynous inner self, has become both more daring and a bit wiser.

In contrast to Lyca is the protagonist of *The Book of Thel* (1789)—the first of Blake's illuminated prophetic books, and one that approaches sublimity. A female counterpart to Tiriel, Thel (whose name is Greek for "wish" or "want") is endowed with a sort of curious timidity.[7] Thel's self-infatuation, paralleling that of Har and Heva, is reflected in her speech—for instance, in her habit of referring to herself by name, in the third person: "Ah! Thel is like a watery bow" (1.8). The limpid flow of the verse, with its wonderfully controlled long line, is also meant to suggest that Thel is a female Narcissus, whose stubborn insistence on preserving her virginity makes her a formidable counterweight to some of Blake's earlier and later androgynous characters. With unconscious irony Thel compares herself to "a parting cloud" (1.8), and her male counterpart in the poem, the "little Cloud" introduced towards the end of part 1, tries to teach her the poem's central message—"every thing that lives / Lives not alone, nor for itself"

(2.26–27)—but he fails, just as Thel fails to achieve her psychic majority. She comes closest to doing so when she sees a Worm in human form—"I see thee like an infant" (3.3)—whose inarticulate weeping appeals to her latent sexual and maternal instincts more powerfully than the Cloud's rhetoric. Like Blake's Tyger, the infant Worm oxymoronically combines life and death, Innocence and Experience.

Thel's failure to grasp the nettle of experience as dramatized not only by the infant Worm but also, more explicitly, by the female Lilly of the valley and Clod of Clay, provokes some of Blake's most memorable verse thus far when she hears a voice "from out the hollow pit" (4.10)—her own grave plot, which ironically is now also her hollow womb:

> Why cannot the Ear be closed to its own destruction?
> Or the glistning Eye to the poison of a smile!
> Why are Eyelids stord with arrows ready drawn,
> Where a thousand fighting men in ambush lie?
> Or an Eye of gifts & graces show'ring fruits & coined gold!
> Why a Tongue impress'd with honey from every wind?
> Why an Ear, a whirlpool fierce to draw creations in?
> Why a nostril wide inhaling terror trembling & affright
> Why a tender curb upon the youthful burning boy!
> Why a little curtain of flesh on the bed of our desire?
>
> The Virgin started from her seat, & with a shriek
> Fled back unhinderd till she came into the vales of Har
>
> (4.11–22)

Lines 19–20, with their daring (for the time) phallic and hymeneal imagery,[8] are the final provocation of Thel's shriek and flight back to the false security of the land where Tiriel too had found no rest. This is liminal verse in which style mirrors content, as Thel's fatal persistence in maintaining her separate, unfulfilled sexuality is unflinchingly yet compassionately lamented by a voice that is at once anonymous—although it maybe that of the matron Clay—and implicitly androgynous, as well as coming from below. One is reminded of the androgynous Jesus portrayed complete with breasts and halo in the illustrations to "The Little Boy Found," and also in Blake's illustration of "Christ descending into the Grave," from his designs to Blair.

The Urizen Myth: Theogony and Androgyny

The mode and motif of the androgynous sublime is maintained throughout Blake's prophecies, although it tends to "go underground" in the revolutionary books of 1790–95. This leitmotif is developed in a minor key, from the portrayal of the failed ménage à trois in *Visions of the Daughters of Albion,* which culminates in Oothoon's great paean of free love, to the Preludium of *America: A Prophecy,* where the shadowy Daughter of Urthona unexpectedly enjoys her brother Orc's "fierce embrace" (1.10)—from a conventional viewpoint, condoning incestuous rape—to the somewhat more enigmatic portrayal of Enitharmon's "crystal house" in *Europe: A Prophecy,* wherein, after awakening from her sleep of eighteen hundred years, Enitharmon calls her sons and daughters to the proto-apocalyptic "sports of night" (12.14). In this probable allusion to the empress Catherine the Great's ice palace, which Cowper had mentioned in *The Task* (5.129ff), Blake's ambiguity need not hide his burgeoning interest in androgyny and its ironic counterparts: compare the literal meaning of the word "womanizer," elaborated on in some of the illustrations to the major prophecies.

Blake seems to be "opening up" here. In the text of the slightly earlier *Marriage of Heaven and Hell,* which has the sulphurous stink and clarion ring of a manifesto, women were conspicuous by their absence, except for one generic but perhaps revealing reference in the Proverbs of Hell: "The nakedness of woman is the work of God" (25). Blake's mention of nakedness here brings to mind one of his less well-known but thematically relevant achievements: for all practical purposes, he was the first English artist to have exploited the nude. His illustrations throughout his career show a healthy appreciation of male and female forms as well as features, based on one of his cardinal principles: "Art & Science cannot exist but by Naked Beauty displayd."[9]

In what is now known as the Urizen trilogy (*The Book of Urizen, The Book of Ahania,* and *The Book of Los*) Blake plunges headlong into the development of his creation myth, which inevitably involves both a kind of theogony as well as the concept of androgyny—original, disrupted, and somehow to be reconstituted. Since *The Book of Urizen* begins in medias res, with Urizen already fallen, Blake's version of the myth of an original androgyne does not get under way until chapter 5, wherein he portrays the creation of Enitharmon, "the first female form now separate" (18:10), from a globe of Los's blood. Los is of course Urizen's antagonist; originally they were a part of the divine unity in which God and Man, as well as males and females, were harmoniously united. This prelapsarian androgynous state is most vividly evoked towards the end of the second part of the trilogy, when Urizen's emanation Ahania poignantly laments their lost paradise:

> Then thou with thy lap full of seed
> With thy hand full of generous fire
> Walked forth from the clouds of morning
> On the virgins of springing joy,
> On the human soul to cast
> The seed of eternal science.

(5:28-34)

The long speech from which this brief excerpt is taken is arguably the most sublime passage in the entire trilogy. As Morton Paley remarks, "Blake follows Boehme, the Kabbala, and the tale of Aristophanes in the Symposium in presenting the androgynous human body as a symbol of libidinal freedom."[10]

The Four Zoas: From Misogyny to Renewed Androgyny

Blake's decision, made some time between 1797 and 1809, to change the title of what was originally "Vala: or the Death and Judgment of the Ancient Man: a DREAM of Nine Nights," to "The Four Zoas: The torments of Love & Jealousy in the Death and Judgment of *Albion* the Ancient Man" involved more than just a textual change: it also suggests an important shift from the perhaps revealing philogyny of his annotations to Lavater to a degree of (temporary) misogyny that cast a deepening shadow over what he refers to as the "twenty dark, but very profitable years" of his middle period, during which he says he was annoyed by a "spectrous Fiend . . . [who] is the enemy of conjugal love."[11] This misogyny is reflected in the fulminations of the Zoas against their emanations and of Albion against Vala, whom he allows to supplant Jerusalem, in the first three Nights of the poem. The quasi-pornographic drawings of the manuscript of *The Four Zoas,* many of which have been partially erased by nineteenth-century bowdlerizers, point in the same direction, and most of the explicitly Christian references are late additions to the poem.[12]

The concept of an original androgynous familial state remains fundamental to Blake's myth in its revised form, albeit he frequently, in common with most of his contemporaries, uses the generic term "Man":

> Then those in Great Eternity met in the Council of God
> As one Man for contracting their Exalted Senses

> They behold Multitude or Expanding they behold as one
> As One Man all the Universal Family & that One Man
> They call Jesus the Christ & they in him & he in them
> Live in Perfect harmony in Eden the land of life
> Consulting as One Man . . .
>
> (1.21:1-6)

Originally Albion was a part or member of this unity, and he comprised four "Zoas" (literally, beasts) or faculties, each with is appropriate emanation or female portion, all the latter making up Albion's emanation, Jerusalem.

Although the poem extends from Albion's fall into time to his regeneration into eternity, the main emphasis falls on the first part of this process, which poet James Reaney has compared to "a cosmic nervous breakdown."[13] Albion's division involves the separation of the Zoas from each other and from their emanations, whereupon they become spectres. The dramatic turning-point of the action comes when Tharmas, the mysterious "parent-power" among the Zoas, recognizes the Spectre of Los as fallen Urthona ["earth-owner"] and restores his emanation Enitharmon to him, so that he can become reintegrated as Los and accomplish the binding of Urizen, or creation of the material world. In binding Urizen Los is also binding a part of himself, so that "Limit / Was put to Eternal Death" (4.53:20–56:24).

The binding of Urizen takes seven ages, each of which Blake calls "a state of dismal woe"—each, that is, except the second. Here Blake is parodying a scholastic tradition that goes back to the Book of Genesis, wherein the second day of creation was the only one God did not deem "good"—according to some commentators, because it was the first one to go beyond unity. Medieval scholars had stigmatized the creation of Eve on similar grounds. In Blake's myth the creation of the natural man (Adam) is a painful but necessary process, so he simply inverts the scholastic convention and in effect anathematizes each of the seven "ages" except the second, which is significantly devoted to the formation of fallen Man's heart—"a red round globe"—and blood vessels (4.54:16–19). The heart is associated with Los's emanation, Enitharmon, who is also formed from a globe of Los's blood. Enitharmon and Luvah ["lover"] are both redemptive principles, and the heart and blood are the life-giving part of fallen Man that will help to work his regeneration, the symbol of which is Christ's incarnation as Orc-Luvah. Thus, when the binding of Urizen is complete, "The Council of God on high watching over the Body / Of Man clothd in Luvahs robes of blood saw & wept" whereupon "the daughters of Beulah saw the Divine Vision they were comforted," having seen in the creation of Man's heart and blood vessels on Los's anvil during the second age the divine mercy and the promise of redemption by the Savior (4.55:10–13).

A second turning-point occurs in Night 7 [A] when Los, fallen Urthona, is reunited with his Spectre and embraces his "real self" (7[A].85:35). This imaginative act of self-forgiveness, hence for-giveness of others, also involves Los's reunion with Enitharmon; thus the motif of renewed androgyny becomes the pivot upon which the poem turns:

> Turn inwardly thine Eyes & there behold the Lamb of God
> Clothd in Luvahs robes of blood descending to redeem
> O Spectre of Urthona take comfort O Enitharmon
> Couldst thou but cease from terror & trembling & affright
> When I appear before thee in forgiveness of ancient injuries
> Why shouldst thou remember & be afraid.
>
> (7[A]. 87:44–49)

Los's words signal a powerful reintegrative momentum that builds up to the sublime climax of Night 9, when the remaining Zoas are likewise reunited with their Emanations and Jerusalem is fully reconstituted, "a City yet a Woman" (9.122:18). The pastoral apocalyptics of the penultimate scene, including a glorious *agape* and a wild bacchanal, culminate in regenerate Albion's acknowl-edgement of his original error and that of his Zoas, particularly Luvah and Vala, or Man's passional instincts (9.126:6–17). All this is meant to express the vision of a world restored, the same and yet different, purged of its major errors. Blake's concept of renewed androgyny emphasizes its imaginative rather than its physical as-pect, without denying the latter, as is indicated in some of the pencil drawings to Night 9, including one showing two figures, male and female, treading grapes, a woman playing a flute, and a feather-cinctured woman with jewels and a tabor, who looks as though she is resting after having enjoyed sexual intercourse.[14]

Milton: Theology versus Androgyny

The first of the major prophecies to be engraved, *Milton* is on the whole a more sublime poem than *The Four Zoas*, although the word *sublime* occurs in it only once, in the Preface. Blake more than makes up for this deficiency, if it is one, in his letters. *Milton* is no doubt the "Sublime Allegory" whose "Authors are in Eternity" that Blake refers to in his letter of 6 July 1803 to Thomas Butts, characteristically adding: "Allegory address'd to the Intellectual powers, while it is altogether hidden from the Corporeal Understanding, is My Definition of the Most Sublime Poetry."[15]

This newfound confidence, which enabled Blake to compare the sublimity of *Milton* to that of the Bible, is also reflected in the text and designs of the poem itself, involving as it does the inspiration of the "Daughters of Beulah" (2.1), as well as the eponymous Puritan poet, whose quarrel with himself the reader readily recognizes:

> Say first! what mov'd Milton, who walked about in Eternity
> One hundred years, pondring the intricate mazes of Providence
> Unhappy tho in heav'n . . .
> Viewing his Sixfold emanation scatter'd thro' the deep
> In torment! To go into the deep her to redeem & himself perish?
>
> (2:16–20)

Milton's problem is the strong element of Calvinism in his theology, with its harsh doctrines of election and predestination, which manifests itself sometimes in a tone of anger and vindictiveness in his late poetry, and—on the psychosexual level—in terms of his separation from his female emanation Ololon, who is described as sixfold because Milton had three wives and three daughters. In other words, Milton's theology needs to be androgynized.

This is the essential burden of the "Bards prophetic Song," beginning "Mark well my words! they are of your [i.e., Milton's] eternal salvation" (2.22ff), which takes up roughly the first half of book 1. This motif is compounded with the matter of the three sons of Los—Rintrah, Palamabron, and Satan—and their emanations, as well as with the business of the three classes of men. Particularly germane to the present study is the delicately adumbrated ménage à quatre involving Satan, his emanation Leutha, and Palamabron and his emanation Elynittria. This psychosexual theme manifests itself as early as Plate 5, when "Satan fainted beneath the arrows of Elynittria" (43), but is not fully developed until plate 13, when the emanations take matters into their own hands:

> But Elynittria met Leutha in the place where she was hidden.
> And threw aside her arrows, and laid down her sounding bow;
> She sooth'd her with soft words & brought her to Palamabrons bed
> In moments new created for delusion, interwoven round about,
> In dreams she bore the shadowy Spectre of Sleep & namd him Death.

In dreams she bore Rahab the mother of Tirzah & her sisters
In Lambeths vales; in Cambridge & in Oxford, places of Thought
Intricate labyrinths of Times and Spaces unknown, that Leutha lived
In Palamabrons Tent, and Oothoon was her charming guard.

(13:36–44)

(Oothoon is Blake's Promethean champion of free love from *Visions of the Daughters of Albion*.) This passage completes the Bard's song, the perception of the truth of which causes Milton to descend from the false security of his heaven in Eternity and become "reborn" in William Blake.

On the biographical level, as I have shown elsewhere, much of this refers to Blake's idea that his patron Hayley (also named "William") had sexual designs on Blake's wife Catherine, and his imaginative efforts to overcome jealousy by the sublimation of art—a theme that is picked up in some of the poem's illustrations, two of which portray homoerotic embraces.[16]

Book 2 opens with a lovely androgynous description of Beulah, into which "the Sons & Daughters of Ololon descended / With solemn mourning . . . / Weeping for Milton" (30:4–6). Milton's present problem is that although he has descended, he has not yet united with his emanation, and hence must remain a spectre until he does so.

Now Ololon continues her descent, following Milton's track into the cracked Mundane Egg. As she looks down into the "Heavens of Ulro" or realm of eternal death, Ololon contrasts the life in the eternal world, where intellectual war and hunting are the two fountains of the river of life, with the corporeal war she sees beneath her. At this point she resembles Thel: but whereas Thel shrieked and drew back into Beulah ("the vales of Har"), Ololon descends, and as Blake says, this is the only way one can ultimately enter Golgonooza, the city of Imagination:

For Golgonooza cannot be seen till having passed the Polypus
It is viewed on all sides round by a Four-fold Vision
Or till you become Mortal & Vegetable in Sexuality
Then you behold its mighty Spires & Domes of ivory & gold

(35:22–25)

Although Blake figuratively refers to Ololon as following Milton's track, of which he helpfully provides an illustration, Susan Fox has observed that "Milton's descent is both simultaneous and identical with Ololon's descent; all the other actions of the poem, past and present, are merely component actions of that focal event."[17] True, the poem's flowerlike structure is based on Blake's concept of opening a center, according to which the poet's work is done "Within a Moment: a Pulsation of the Artery" (29:3). But Fox, who elsewhere criticizes Blake's fulminations against the "Female Will," about which much has been written, fails to note that in portraying Ololon's descent sequentially after Milton's, he is really emphasizing her spiritual autonomy:

> There is a Moment in each Day that Satan cannot find
> Nor can his Watch Fiends find it, but the Industrious find
> This Moment & it multiply. & when it once is found
> It renovates every Moment of the Day if rightly placed[.]
> In this Moment Ololon descended to Los & Enitharmon
> Unseen beyond the Mundane Shell Southward in Miltons track
>
> (35:42–47)

Ololon next appears in Blake's garden at Felpham as a virgin of twelve years. There is Blakean humor in this, as one is invited to ask oneself what one would do if suddenly confronted by a twelve-year-old virgin descending into one's garden. One of the advantages of reading Blake is that one learns how to handle such situations: he addresses her courteously and invites her into his cottage to comfort his wife (who was ill at the time), presumably over a cup of tea. But Ololon scarcely has time for such niceties:

> The Virgin answered. Knowest thou of Milton who descended
> Driven from Eternity; him I seek! terrified at my Act
> In Great Eternity which thou knowest! I come him to seek
>
> (37:1–3)

Ololon's "Act"—her voluntary descent into "death in Ulro among the Transgressors" (21:46)—was itself prefigured by that of Leutha in offering herself as a "Ransom for Satan, taking on his Sin" (11:30), which led to the imaginative ménage à quatre discussed previously. So the motif of imaginative androgyny is woven into the rich fabric of the poem, intertwined with the related idea that "The Sexual is Threefold: the Human Fourfold" (4:5). Accordingly Ololon must also put off her errors, ironically symbolized by her virginity, counterpart to the negative side of Milton's Puritanism.

Milton's theology has now been replaced by sublime androgyny, and "All Animals upon the Earth, are prepared in all their strength / To go forth to the Great Harvest & Vintage of the Nations." (42:39–43:1) The illustration of the last plate shows Ololon standing naked, having put off her veil of virginity, with arms outstretched, flanked by two figures, one male and one androgynous, symbolizing the human harvest to come.

Jerusalem: The Androgynous Sublime

Jerusalem: The Emanation of the Giant Albion, the last and greatest of Blake's major prophecies, is also, as its title suggests, the most explicitly androgynous. Morton Paley has observed that among the precedents for Blake's Albion, the Universal Man of whom we all members, is the androgynous one depicted in the frontispiece to Michael Drayton's *Poly-Olbion* (1622), who later undergoes a sex change and begets three children by the river Poole.[18] In Blake's myth Albion's troubles began as a sort of wet dream when an "Aged Woman [who] is Brittannica the Wife of Albion," "divided into Jerusalem & Vala."[19] Among the other precursors of Blake's Albion I have identified Shakespeare's portrayal in *King Lear* of the Duke of Albany, whose initial "milky gentleness," as Goneril scornfully calls it, as well as his dramatic transformation toward the end of the play, seems to have influenced Blake's symbolism.[20]

Comprising one hundred plates divided into four roughly equal parts addressed to the public, the Jews, the deists, and the Christians respectively, *Jerusalem* has as its ethical and imaginative base the proposition that "The Spirit of Jesus is continual forgiveness of Sins" (3:Preface). W. H. Auden has observed that "Every beautiful poem presents an analogy to the forgiveness of sins."[21] This is a statement that Blake would have approved but found reversible: every imaginative act of forgiveness helps to build up Golgonooza, the palace of art whose human form is Jerusalem.

The Savior whom Blake now sees "Spreading his beams of love, & dictating the words of this mild song" (4:5) is implicitly androgynous, harking back to the sacramental sublime of "To Spring." The Savior calls upon Albion to awake, and asks him, "Where hast thou hidden thy Emanation lovely Jerusalem / From the vision and fruition of the Holy-one?" (4:16–17). What follows is the "perturbed Man" Albion's persistence in his willful transvaluation of values, including the introduction of "Laws of Moral Virtue" and his domination by Urizen, "hiding [Albion's] emanation" in the darkness of jealousy (4:21–33). Albion's separation from Jerusalem is reflected in the division of his twelve sons from their emanations—a division that in turn reflects what I have elsewhere referred to as the poem's antithetical structure.[22] Since I there focused my attention on the quasi-autobiographical role of Albion's sons, most of whom were involved in Blake's trial for sedition, my present endeavor will be to right the balance by paying primary attention to Albion's daughters, bearing in mind that Blake's drive is always toward imaginative androgyny:

> The Male is a Furnace of beryll; the Female is a golden Loom;
> I behold them and their rushing fires overwhelm my Soul,
> In Londons darkness; and my tears fall day and night,
> Upon the Emanations of Albions Sons! the Daughters of Albion
> Names anciently remembered, but now contemn'd as fictions!
> Although in every bosom they controll our Vegetative powers.
>
> (5:34–39)

Five of Albion's daughters—"Cambel & Gwendolen & Conwenna & Cordella & Ignoge"—are united into Tirzah ["teazer"], a name first mentioned in "To Tirzah," a late (c.1801) addition to the *Songs of Experience.* The remaining seven—"Gwiniverra & Gwinifred & Goneril & Sabrina beautiful, / Estrid, Mehetabel & Ragan" (5:41–44)—combine into Rahab, for whose twofold function (as aider of the Israelites and ancestress of Jesus on the one hand, and prototype of the Great Whore of Revelation on the other) there is ample biblical precedent.[23] Blake saw these two female types—the Virgin and the Whore—as alternating from one age to another. In his painting *The Canterbury Pilgrims,* later engraved, the Prioress, who represents Tirzah, is contrasted with the Wife of Bath, representing Rahab. After praising the Prioress's beauty, Blake remarks of these two that they are equally "a scourge and a blight"—a statement that must be seen in light of his doctrine of the importance of distinguishing between states and individuals of those states.[24] In common with current feminist theory, Blake is objecting to the artificial bifurcation of women into these two superficially opposite but fundamentally similar archetypes (Tirzah is Rahab's daughter).

Jerusalem's antithetical structure is also reflected, inevitably, in Los's separation from Enitharmon and his efforts to subdue his Spectre so that he can become reintegrated with her, thus acting as a sort of "mini-Albion," or precursor of universal regeneration. Los, with whom Blake now identifies more closely than ever, succeeds so heroically in this enterprise that he is later praised by the Sons of Eden for keeping "the Divine Vision in time of trouble" (44:15).

There is a timeless quality about *Jerusalem* that makes it read rather like a more sober version of *Finnegans Wake*—which it influenced—as when Los, taking a panoramic view of history, tells his now-obedient Spectre he saw "Every Emanative joy forbidden as a Crime: . . . Inspiration deny'd; Genius forbidden by laws of punishment!" (9:14–16). Accordingly Los says he took the tears and groans and sighs of the victims and lifted them into his furnace "to form the spiritual sword / That lays open the hidden heart," heating his anvil "Nine times" (no doubt a reference to the nine Nights of *The Four Zoas*) until

> Gwendolen & Cambel & Gwineverra
> Are melted into the gold, the silver, the liquid ruby,
> The crysolite, the topaz, the jacinth, & every precious stone.
> (9:18–24)

Here the intertextual reference seems to be to Blake's manuscript poem "The Mental Traveller," which ironically portrays a threefold world of cyclical recurrence in which the sexes are perpetually at odds with each other, causing endless strife:

> And these are the gems of the Human Soul
> The rubies & pearls of a lovesick eye
> The countless gold of the akeing heart
> The martyrs groan & the lovers sigh
> (33–36)

The passage from *Jerusalem* continues with an account of Los transforming the passions into works of art, thus "building Golgonooza" (10:17) between the Scylla of the sexual games of Albion's daughters and the Charybdis of the abstract reasoning of his sons.

Encouraging Los in his work is the appearance of Erin, the spiritual form of Ireland, who now comes forth from his furnaces, followed by "all the Daughters of Beulah" (11:8). Insofar as Erin represents what Damon calls Blake's "philosophy of love,"[25] like the earlier Oothoon she probably is based partly on Mary Wollstonecraft, advocate of free love and author of *The Rights of Woman*, who was of Irish extraction and whom we know Blake admired. The Spaces of Erin, reaching "from the starry height, to the starry depth" (12:23), are implicitly contrasted—poets need space[26]—to the Veil of Vala, the latter being a delusive form of the fallen world obscuring Jerusalem.

Golgonooza is new Golgotha, and in it all history is redeemed of its errors and perceived in its eternal aspect, as a work of art. Although Blake says both Los's sons and daughters are involved in its construction, the specific reference to two of the latter—Erin and Ethinthus—is meant to suggest the martyrdom of women and men's tenderer feelings throughout most of what passes for human history:

> What are those golden builders doing? where was the burying-place
> Of soft Ethinthus? near Tyburns fatal Tree? is that
> Mild Zions hills most ancient promontory: near mournful
> Ever weeping Paddington? Is that Calvary and Golgotha?
> Becoming a building of pity and compassion? Lo!
> The stones are pity, and the bricks, well wrought affections:
> Enameld with love & kindness, & the tiles engraven gold
> Labour of merciful hands: the beams & rafters are forgiveness:
> The mortar & cement of the work, tears of honesty: the nails,
> And the screws & iron braces, are well wrought blandishments,
> And well contrived words, firm fixing, never forgotten,
> Always comforting the remembrance: the floors, humility,
> The cielings, devotion: the hearths, thanksgiving . . .
>
> (12:25–37)

This is followed by a favorable, punning reference to "Lambeth [whom] the bride of the Lambs Wife" (12:41) loves—that is, the district of London on the south side of the Thames where the Blakes had issued their "Lambeth books" (*America* through *Ahania*), and where the foundations of Jerusalem, the oxymoronic ravished Bride, were "laid in ruins" (*M,* 6:14–15), as well as, doubtless, those of *Jerusalem*.[27] As Marney Ward has observed, although "Jerusalem is called Liberty among the [fallen] Children of Albion" (54:5), she really represents forgiveness.[28]

The account of Los's halls in Golgonooza is in a similar vein:

> All things acted on earth are seen in the bright Sculptures of
> Los's Halls & every Age renews its powers from these Works
> With every pathetic story possible to happen from Hate or
> Wayward Love & every sorrow & distress is carved here
> Every Affinity of Parents Marriages & Friendships are here
> In all their various combinations wrought with wondrous Art
> All that can happen to Man in his pilgrimage of seventy years.
>
> (16:61–67)

In both passages Blake is assuming the androgynous character of the artist *qua* artist.

In plate 17 Enitharmon divides from Los: Blake is moving "backward" here, all events being simultaneous from the sublime perspective of Los's halls. Returning in this unexpected way to the myth of Albion's fall, Blake tells how Vala, originally the garment of God, seduced Albion "to destroy Jerusalem" with her false love, "which separated the stars from the mountains: the mountains from Man / And left Man, a little grovelling Root, outside of Himself" (17:31–32), whereupon Vala became Nature, mother of all, with her daughters Rahab and Tirzah. Albion's sons meanwhile petrify and become a "Satanic Mill! . . . ravning to gormandize" Albion's sleeping humanity (19:19–23).

At this low point, when Albion's "Circumference was clos'd; [and] his Center began darkning," the moon of Beulah arises and Los finds

> Jerusalem upon the River of his City soft repos'd
> In the arms of Vala, assimilating in one with Vala
> The Lilly of Havilah.
>
> (19:36–43)

This lesbian embrace, corresponding to the homoerotic embraces portrayed in *Milton,* is the hidden turning-point of *Jerusalem*—hidden, insofar as the type of love it portrays was considered illicit.

Following this encounter, when Vala speaks of shame and Jerusalem of forgiveness, the latter moves to the poem's dramatic center:

> O Vala what is Sin? that thou shudderest and weepest
> At sight of thy once lov'd Jerusalem! what is Sin but a little
> Error & fault that is soon forgiven . . .
>
> (20.22–24)

With artful juxtaposition, Blake illustrates this pivotal scene in plate 28, which begins chapter 2, suggesting, among other things, that Jerusalem and Vala are ahead of their time.

This plate has bemused Blake scholars. For awhile there was a brisk debate over whether the couple are both female, or male and female. In an early version of the plate the lovers are placed in a position that definitely suggests copulation and hence implies two sexes.[29] But as Erdman points out, Blake revised this plate considerably from its proof state. "At first the embracing pair were male (at left) and female; they now seem to fit the references to Jerusalem [and Vala]." The short hair of the figure on the right, against the backdrop of Vala's enormous (as well as eponymous) veil, now being put off, plus a few phallic remnants from the proof noted by Erdman, continue to develop the motif of intimations of sublime androgyny.[30]

As in Shelley's *Prometheus Unbound,* the dramatic turning point, which in both poems comes fairly early, is followed by events

Plate 28 of *Jerusalem* (Copy E) showing the lesbian embrace of Jerusalem and Vala.

that seem to belie it. Chapter 2 antithetically opens with Albion
assuming the role of "punisher & judge" (that is, still under the
domination of his spectre) and condemning "unnatural consangui-
nites and friendships / Horrid to think of when enquired deeply
into" (28:7–8). Thus Albion turns his back to the Divine Vision,
whereupon Vala reveals that she became "Albions Bride & Wife
in great Eternity" after emanating from Luvah, despite the fact
that, as Albion reminds her, "In Eternity they neither marry nor
are given in marriage" (29:1–30:15). Before she became Albion's
bride, Vala was a part of Jerusalem; afterward, she created the
state of love divided from imagination that is the antithesis of universal brotherhood and the hermaphroditic opposite to imaginative
androgyny. Some of the Eternals (presumably males) have a good
laugh over Albion's predicament:

> Have you known the Judgment that is arisen among the
> Zoas of Albion? where a Man dare hardly to embrace
> His own Wife, for the terrors of Chastity that they call
> By the name of Morality.
>
> (32:44–47)

This is followed by an abortive, because premature, attempt on
the part of the Divine Family—presumably initiated by the females—to bear Albion "in love sublime, &, as on Cherubs wings"
(39:1) back to Eden, suggesting that some sort of family discussion
has been going on among the Eternals, paralleling the turmoil on
earth. As in Milton's portrayal of the prelapsarian relations of
Adam and Eve, Blake's concept of Edenic androgyny evidently
does not preclude lively debate.

Albion's Western Gate—his empathic sense of touch, identified
in the poem's symbolism with the city of Bath—is at this point
closed, in spite of the best efforts of certain poets and preachers
"whose Western Gates were open" (40:34), and who were currently
speaking out, in Bath and elsewhere, against such errors as the
slave trade and the war with France.[31] Blake's Western Gate symbolism comes to a climax toward the end of this chapter with the
reappearance of Erin as "an Aged pensive Woman," whose "sublime shade" the Daughters of Beulah embrace (48:28–29). Erin's
long speech, reflecting Blake's interest in Catholic emancipation
and the devolution of power away from the imperial center, also
implicitly prophesies the opening of Albion's Western Gate by
mentioning "the golden Gate of Havilah" (49:15), a conflation of
the biblical Havilah (Gen. 2.11); Avalon, the Celtic paradise; and

Avila, a center of Spanish mysticism. (Compare the Spanish influence on Ireland's western port city of Galway, birthplace of Nora Joyce, and the Gibraltar mentioned in Molly Bloom's final soliloquy in *Ulysses*.) All this suggests the quietism of the later Blake's politics, as well as the idea of the liberation of the senses, hence imaginative androgyny.

In chapter 3 the Daughters of Albion assume the ascendancy and engage in an extraordinary Walpurgis Night of human sacrifice, in which Blake conflates modern warfare with Druidism, symbolic counterpart of the mental outlook of the deists to whom this chapter is addressed. In contrast to the androgynous sublime, Blake emphasizes the basis of such sadism in frustrated sexuality, as Albion's daughters dance "Naked & drunk" while his sons "bonify," sacrifice Luvah, and become hermaphroditic spectres (58:2–20).

Antithetical to this résumé of the nightmare of history is Los's evocation "in the Visions of Elohim Jehovah" (61:2) of the conception of Jesus, which came about when Mary, "ignorant of crime in the midst of a corrupt Age,"[32] yielded to the impulse of true desire. Mary's Oothoon-like passionate activity, and Joseph's compassion, once he has overcome his anger, make them both sublime figures, whose mingling of spirits illustrates not only Blake's doctrine of forgiveness as the sine qua non of Christianity, but also his well-placed Edenic vision of imaginative androgyny, wherein "Embraces are Cominglings: from the Head even to the Feet; / And not a pompous High Priest entering by a Secret Place" (69:43–44).

Blake dovetails the two main themes of this chapter—the androgynous character of Jesus and the crucifixion of Luvah, who "is France" (66:15)—by artfully juxtaposing the text and designs of plates 62 and 63, the text dealing with the former theme, and the designs with the latter. The illustration of plate 62 shows Luvah with his head bound by a brazen serpent, which is both a symbol of Jesus and a visual pun on the phrase "serpent temple."[33] Between Luvah's feet at the bottom of the page Los appears as a tiny form, witnessing the crucifixion of Luvah-France by British imperial war policy.

In the following plate Luvah's emanation Vala appears as a reclining nude with shorn hair, crossed legs, and her loins caught in the coils of a huge live worm. Earlier in the poem Blake gave France a "Masculine Emanation" named Shiloh, the only male "among the flowers of Beulah" (49:47), a reference to the fact that during this period the practice of male homosexuality—more precisely, sodomy—was a hanging offense in England, but was permit-

Jehovah stood among the Druids in the Valley of Annandale
When the Four Zoas of Albion, the Four Living Creatures, the Cherubim
Of Albion tremble before the Spectre, in the Starry Harness of the Plow
Of Nations. And their Names are Urizen & Luvah & Tharmas & Urthona
Luvah slew Tharmas the Angel of the Tongue & Albion brought him
To Justice in his own City of Paris, denying the Resurrection
Then Vala the Wife of Albion, who is the Daughter of Luvah
Took vengeance Twelve-fold among the Chaotic Rocks of the Druids
Where the Human Victims howl to the Moon & Thor & Friga
Dance the dance of death contending with Jehovah among the Cherubim
The Chariot Wheels filled with Eyes rage along the howling Valley
In the Dividing of Reuben & Benjamin bleeding from Chesters River

The Giants & the Witches & the Ghosts of Albion dance with
Thor & Friga, & the Fairies lead the Moon along the Valley of Cherubim
Bleeding in torrents from Mountain to Mountain. a lovely Victim
And Jehovah stood in the Gates of the Victim. & he appeared
A weeping Infant in the Gates of Birth in the midst of Heaven

The Cities & Villages of Albion became Rock & Sand Unhumanized
The Druid Sons of Albion & the Heavens a Void around unfathomable
No Human Form but Sexual & a little weeping Infant pale reflected
Multitudinous in the Looking Glass of Enitharmon on all sides
Around in the clouds of the Female, on Albions Cliffs of the Dead

Such the appearance in Cheviot: in the Divisions of Reuben

When the Cherubim hid their heads under their wings in deep slumbers
When the Druids demanded Chastity from Woman & all was lost.

How can the Female be Chaste O thou stupid Druid Cried Los
Without the Forgiveness of Sins in the merciful clouds of Jehovah
And without the Baptism of Repentance to wash away Calumnies. and
The Accusations of Sin that each may be Pure in their Neighbours sight
O, when shall Jehovah give us Victims from his Flocks & Herds
Instead of Human Victims by the Daughters of Albion & Canaan

Then laugh'd Gwendolen & her laughter shook the Nations & Families of
The Dead beneath Beulah from Tyburn to Golgotha. and from
Ireland to Japan, furious her Lions & Tygers & Wolves sport before
Los on the Thames & Medway. London & Canterbury groan in pain

Los knew not yet what was done: he thought it was all in Vision
In Visions of the Dreams of Beulah among the Daughters of Albion
Therefore the Murder was put apart in the Looking Glass of Enitharmon
He saw in Vala's hand the Druid Knife of Revenge & the Poison Cup
Of Jealousy, and thought it a Poetic Vision of the Atmospheres
Till Canaan rolld apart from Albion across the Rhine along the Danube

And all the Land of Canaan suspended over the Valley of Cheviot
From Bashan to Tyre & from Troy to Gaza of the Amalekite
And Reuben fled with his head downwards among the Caverns

Plate 63 of *Jerusalem* (Copy C) showing Vala with shorn locks.

ted in France.[34] Hence the sexual ambivalence of Vala's shorn locks in this complementary illustration.

The appearance towards the end of this chapter of Rahab, a "Three-fold Wonder" representing nature's terrible female will in isolation (70:20–31), is followed antithetically by the struggle to emerge of Dinah, "the youthful form of Erin" (74:54). Dinah was a daughter of Leah and Jacob whose lover, Shechem, was killed by her brothers (Gen. 34). Thus, like the earlier Oothoon, she represents the imaginative form of all that is opposed to natural morality, including that of the ultrasexist Rahab, encourager of prostitution and "Religion hid in War" (75:20).

What I referred to near the beginning of this chapter as the transcendentally homoerotic lyric "England! awake!" prefaces chapter 4 of *Jerusalem*. Its theme is the restoration of the temporal to the eternal world seen as the loving reunion of two sisters, the "two virginities" whose coming together will produce the celestial harvest.[35] As this chapter gets underway, Cambel and Gwendolen assume the roles of Rahab and Tirzah, binding Hand and Hyle on the stems of generation with warfare and corporeal sacrifice, until Gwendolen utters her famous "Falsehood" concerning the inefficacy of forgiveness and draws aside her veil, exposing her perfect body to her sisters and "Hyle a winding Worm beneath her" (82:8–47). Cambel, who had assumed the *Venus pudica* pose in plate 81, tries something similar with Hand, but at this low point Gwendolen, howling in torment, repents her plot and begins "her dolorous task of love in the Wine-press of Luvah / to form the Worm into a form of love by tears & pain" (82:75–76). Her sisters behold and weep. One is reminded of the "Infant Worm" in the *The Book of Thel*, likewise a pivotal figure uniting life and death. This second turning point is attributable to genuine repentance and an upsurge of feeling on the part of Gwendolen and her sisters, illustrating once more the subtle shift of emphasis from male to female figures as the poem's redemptive phase gathers momentum.

Los, like the other males, is now tormented by ungratified desire, the suspension of sexual relations being a necessary prelude to the apocalypse, as Blake had cryptically indicated in an earlier manuscript poem beginning "My Spectre around me night & day," which most of his commentators have avoided like the plague:

> Let us agree to give up Love
> And root up the infernal grove
> Then shall we return & see
> the worlds of happy Eternity

(49–52)

Now the daughters of Albion call on Los to come forth with his globe of fire, as depicted in the frontispiece, a globe that is at once an engraver's device for magnifying light and a symbol of the spiritual sun as the source of the poetic genius. Los then sings of his prophetic vision of "the New Jerusalem descending out of Heaven" (86:19) prepared as a bride for her husband. This is followed by a discussion between Los and Enitharmon in which the latter expresses her jealousy of Jerusalem, adding "This is Woman's World" (88:16)—all of which seems at once prophetic and somehow rooted in the domestic life of the Blakes.

In plate 89 Hand appears as the Covering Cherub, Antichrist, in a passage whose uncertain syntax, rather reminding one of Milton's account of Chaos, reflects its "indefinite" content:

> Tho divided by the Cross & Nails & Thorn & Spear
> In Cruelties & Rahab & Tirzah [,] permanent endure
> A terrible indefinite Hermaphroditic form
> A Wine-Press of Love & Wrath double Hermaph[r]oditic
>
> (89:1–4)

This hermaphroditic Antichrist, whose "Brain incloses a reflexion / of Eden all perverted" (89:14–15), is antithetical to the imaginative androgyny of Eden, just as Blake had earlier distinguished between "Comingling / Of Albions & Luvahs Spectres [which] was Hermaphroditic" (58:19–20) and Edenic embraces "from the Head even to the Feet" (69:43).

Rahab now appears as a "Double Female" (89:52) in the devouring monster's stomach, an apparition that has a rhetorical as well as a sexual implication:

> The Feminine separates from Masculine & both from Man,
> Ceasing to be His Emanations, Life to Themselves assuming!
> . . . [until] no more the Masculine mingles
> With the Feminine, but the Sublime is shut out from the Pathos
> In howling torment, to build stone walls of separation, compelling
> The Pathos, to weave curtains of hiding secresy from the torment.
>
> (90:1–13)

In Eden, as most often in Blake's art, the sublime and the pathos (traditionally masculine and feminine) were united; now they are hopelessly sundered.[36]

At this new low point Los denounces the world's leading errors, including "a Vegetated Christ & a Virgin Eve," as part of the "Hermaphroditic / Blasphemy" that now becomes "One Great Satan"

(90:34–43), and is seen to include all forms of corporeal as opposed to spiritual friendship (91:15–17). The appearance of what Los calls "this Body of Doubt that Seems but is Not" (93:20) is a necessary consolidation of error preceding the final apocalypse, which takes place when Albion's children return to his loins and "England, who is Brittannia" (94:20) awakens on his bosom. Albion now also awakens and is reunited with his emanation, who "entered [his] bosom rejoicing, / Rejoicing in his indignation! adoring his wrathful rebuke" (95:22–23) for having divided into Jerusalem and Vala.

Blake devotes three of his last seven plates—94, 96, and 99— to portraying the embraces of Albion and Brittannia, whom Los-Blake recognizes as Jerusalem. Plate 94 shows the aged Albion embraced by England horizontally on the battlefield, like the slain Arthur, which contrasts with the view of them rising together (pl. 96), she with her legs still crossed and looking (as Erdman puts it) "surprised that he is not dead."[37] In plate 99, by contrast, Jerusalem-Vala-England-Everywoman and Jesus-Jehovah-Albion-Everyman improve upon this time for embracing, he still clothed in a loose-fitting gown, she nude and with her arms ecstatically extended. He has his hands on her lower back and wears a curiously doleful expression. They are portrayed amid ascending flames, and his head is surrounded by a dark halo. *She* now seems to be forgiving *him*.

Erdman observes that "the repainting of their faces in [Copy] E . . . seems to make both more male than female." He also notes that "etched on the plate, and visible in [copies] A, C, and posthumous copies, but carefully deleted in others, is a small book in which [Jehovah-Albion] holds his left index finger even while embracing [Jerusalem's] lumbar loins."[38] This bold iconographic stroke I take to be an allusion to the apocalyptic improvement of sensual enjoyment that Blake had prophesied in *The Marriage of Heaven and Hell*, as well as Los's proleptic remark in chapter 2 of *Jerusalem* that "Albion hath entered the Loins the place of the Last Judgment" (44:38).

The last, retrospective illustration occupying all of plate 100 shows Los holding his hammer and compasslike tongs, flanked on either side by his sun-shouldering spectre, who is about to take off, and the moon-controlling Enitharmon, with the "all wondrous Serpent [temple] . . . Humanize[d]" (98:44) in the background— humanized, insofar as it iconographically recapitulates the biblical motif of Alpha and Omega, with a slightly flattened version of the former suggested by Blake's flowing serpent temple (cf. the curvilinear "A" in "Albion," plate 2), and the latter emphasized by

Plate 99 of *Jerusalem* (Copy C) showing Albion and Jerusalem embracing.

Plate 100 of *Jerusalem* (Copy E) showing Los flanked by his spectre and Enitharmon.

its centrality in the design, thus inverting plate 1, which visually stresses the alphalike arch more so than the low-slung engraver's ball (of "golden string," plate 77).[39]

In addition to this visual sublimity, plate 100 also has several intimations of androgyny. Los's genitals, missing or fudged in some copies, are restored in Copy E, while Enitharmon has modish short hair, although it seems to wind around her neck in a double braid. Like Los's spectre, she is seen from the rear, albeit we see her somewhat androgynous profile as she stands (like Los) with her weight on her right foot. Her extended arms rather resemble those of Jerusalem in the previous plate. One tip of the compass-tongs Los is loosely holding in his left hand almost touches his left foot, and the other *does* touch the tip of Enitharmon's left foot—a possible allusion to the compass imagery in John Donne's "A Valediction Forbidding Mourning," and if so, Blake's "left-handed" but doubtless sincere tribute to his marriage to Catherine as a stabilizing force in his life, in what amounts to this valedictory mythic statement, at once imaginatively androgynous and sublime.[40]

2

Wordsworth and the Patriarchal Sublime

A Poetical Adam

THE STANCE WORDSWORTH ADOPTS IN *LYRICAL BALLADS* (1798) is that of a poetical Adam sans Eve, seeing the world for the first time and describing it simply, without adornment. Thus in "Epostulation and Reply" his friend Matthew remarks:

> 'You look round you on your Mother Earth,
> 'As if she for no purpose bore you;
> 'As if you were her first-born birth,
> 'And none had lived before you!'
>
> (9–12)[1]

Undergirding this poetical revolution in stance and style—the latter fully elaborated in the famous Preface to the second edition of *Lyrical Ballads*—was Wordsworth's recent, passionate involvement in and disillusionment with the French Revolution, including his love affair with Annette Vallon, from which he was struggling to salvage something of enduring literary merit. This process can be seen reflected in the following stanza from a poem addressed to his sister Dorothy ("To My Sister"):

> No joyless forms shall regulate
> Our living calendar:
> We from to-day, my Friend, will date
> The opening of the year.
>
> (17–20)

These lines echo the new Republican calendar and the new system of measurement of time introduced by the National Convention during the first few years of the French Revolution, which advocates of the new calendar meant to strike a blow at the clergy and to abolish the Christian year. The new calendar became law on 5

49

October 1793, and remained in effect until 1805. It was also proposed to divide the day on the decimal system, making the smallest unit of time equivalent to the pulse-beat of a man of average stature, but this arrangement was never put into practice. (Compare Blake's *Milton* 28:47ff.)

Hence Wordsworth's antinomian and poetically republican stance when he proclaimed these lines to Dorothy, whose relationship with him, aptly described by the late Kenneth Clark as "Platonic incest,"[2] was itself somewhat revolutionary. The new calendar was regarded as beginning on 22 September 1792, this day being chosen because on it the Republic was proclaimed and because it was the day of the autumnal equinox. When Wordsworth tells Dorothy, "We from to-day, my Friend, will date / The opening of the year" he is referring nominally to the vernal equinox, which in 1798 was actually on 21 March, beginning the month called "Germinal" in the revolutionary calendar; he is really, of course, referring to a kind of poetical rebirth roughly equivalent to what Blake calls the "Eternal Now."[3]

This desire to begin anew may be regarded as Wordsworth's revenge on the French Revolution, as *Paradise Lost* was Milton's revenge on the Commonwealth. Like his admired Milton, though more latently, Wordsworth had a religious agenda that he was playing down during the period of composition of *Lyrical Ballads,* except for the occasional reference to God, as in the poems "We Are Seven" (51) and "The Idiot Boy" (200), such references usually being expressed by female characters. Insofar as the "God" referred to is implicitly patriarchal, this may point to a lingering split between the "masculine" or revolutionary and "feminine" or acquiescent sides of Worthsworth's psyche. Later in Wordsworth's poetic development references to God tend to be expressed by male characters, a well-known example being the concluding couplet of "Resolution and Independence" (1802): "'God,' said I, 'be my help and stay secure; / I'll think of the Leech-gatherer on the lonely moor!'"

The Aqueous and Admonitory Sublime

Wordsworth's first sublime poem in the conventional sense of the word is "Tintern Abbey," of which he said not a word was written down until several days after it was composed during a walking tour with Dorothy in July 1798. Related to the circumstances of the poem's composition is its powerful auditory appeal, signalled by means of imitative harmony:

> and again I hear
> These waters, *rolling* from their mountain-springs
> With a soft inland *murmur.*
>
> > (2–4; emphasis added)

The thematic relevance of this is picked up in some later lines describing the poem's central mystical experience:

> A motion and a spirit, that impels
> All thinking things, all objects of all thought,
> And *rolls* through all things.
>
> > (100–2; emphasis added)

The last section of the poem, which contains some of its finest poetry, is addressed to Dorothy, whose voice is thus described in *The Prelude:*

> Then it was—
> Thanks to the bounteous Giver of all good!—
> That the beloved Sister in whose sight
> Those days were passed, now speaking in a voice
> Of sudden admonition—like a brook
> That did but *cross* a lonely road, and now
> Is seen, heard, felt, and caught at every turn,
> Companion never lost through many a league—
> Maintained for me a saving intercourse
> With my true self . . .
>
> > (11.333–42)

The second of these lines plays upon the fact that "Dorothy" means "gift of God," and the passage goes on to compare the sound of her admonitory voice to that of a brook, reminding the reader that Dorothy's voice was probably the only one heard by Wordsworth at any length during the period of composition of "Tintern Abbey." The fact that Wordsworth italicizes the word *cross* signals both Dorothy's gentle but firm admonition, the suggestion being that she is no real impediment to his true progress, and may also have latently Christian connotations: like Coleridge, Dorothy was destined to undergo a sort of psychic crucifixion on behalf of Wordsworth's career as a poet.

What Dorothy is admonishing her brother about becomes clear in the sequel:

> for, though bedimmed and changed
> Much, as it seemed, I was no further changed

Than as a clouded and a waning moon.

(11.342–44)

There can be little doubt that Dorothy, who at the time referred to knew of her brother's affair with Annette and the birth of their child, was thinking of the effects of this on his psyche:

She whispered still that brightness would return,
She, in the midst of all, preserved me still
A Poet, made me seek beneath that name,
And that alone, my office upon earth.

(11.345–48)

To the extent that moon imagery, which had been associated with Dorothy in one of the most sublime passages of "Tintern Abbey"— the one beginning "Therefore let the moon / Shine on thee in thy solitary walk" (134–35)—is transferred to Wordsworth in these lines from *The Prelude,* something androgynous is in fact going on: a reversal of roles, as Dorothy (who was two years younger than her brother) becomes Wordsworth's tutelary spirit. Moon and water imagery usually has some such latently androgynous as well as mystical (hence potentially sublime) connotations.

The aqueous and admonitory sublime is also heard and felt in one of Wordsworth's most famous sonnets, written shortly after he and Dorothy had paid a brief visit across the Channel to Annette and her and Wordsworth's daughter, Anne-Caroline, beginning:

It is a beauteous evening, calm and free,
The holy time is quiet as a Nun
Breathless with adoration; the broad sun
Is sinking down in its tranquillity;
The gentleness of heaven broods o'er the Sea;
Listen! the mighty Being is awake,
And doth with his eternal motion make
A sound like thunder—everlastingly.

(1–8; emphasis added)

In the last three lines of the octave, Wordsworth is of course refer-ring on the literal level to the sound of the waves breaking on the French coast. But these lines, their outward calm notwithstanding, also reflect Wordsworth's continuing inner tumult over his aban-donment of Annette and their daughter, while on the admonitory and anagogic level they refer to certain passages from the Book of Revelation describing the returned Christ, which seem to have haunted Wordsworth's imagination throughout his most creative period. The passages read in part:

His head and his hairs were white like wool, as white as snow; and his eyes were as flames of fire;
And his feet like unto fine brass, as if they burned in a furnace; *and his voice as the sound of many waters.*
And he had in his right hand seven stars: and out of his mouth went a sharp twoedged sword: *and his countenance was As the sun shineth in his strength* . . . (1: 14–16; emphasis added)

And I heard a voice from heaven, as the voice of many waters, and as the voice of a great thunder . . . (14: 2; emphasis added)

And I heard as it were the voice of a great multitude, and *as the voice of many waters, and as the voice of mighty thunderings* . . .

(19: 6; emphasis added)

The opening lines of the sonnet, including the comparison of "the holy time" to "a Nun," help to establish the religious frame of reference, which is further developed by the implicit comparison via Revelation 1:16 of the (setting) sun to the face of God. The most powerful trope, however, is the auditory one, with the sound of waves breaking on the French coast, where Wordsworth was walking with his natural daughter, being compared to the thundering voice of the returned Christ. The image suggests the unity of human, natural, and patriarchal divine "voice" that eighteenth-century Hebraists claimed to have found in the original language of the Old Testament.[4]

This thundering, patriarchal voice, whose reverberations are heard throughout Wordsworth's poetry, usually in association with water imagery, presents a marked contrast to the murmuring and androgynous voices of the rivers Wye and Derwent, as well as of Dorothy. The former is meant to be "sublime" and the latter "beautiful," in accordance with the dichotomy postulated by Edmund Burke, who associated sublimity with "the large and the gigantic," as well as with terror, and beauty with "littleness."[5] Thus the octave of the sonnet, beginning with the trope of the silent Nun and proceeding to that of the thunderous voice of God, is an extended oxymoron, which would be androgynous if it were not for the imbalance suggested by the muting (i.e., neutering) of the Nun.

The implied admonition and self-judgment comes through in the buried allusions to the passages from Revelation I have indicated, but these are subsumed within a context of acceptance in the sestet, with its reference to "Abraham's bosom," a biblical metaphor for God, and the assertion that Wordsworth's French daughter, whom he both acknowledges and does *not* acknowledge, is closer to God than he is. The use of the word *broods* in line 5 ("The gentleness of heaven *broods* o'er the sea") echoes Milton's reference to the creation in the opening verse paragraph of *Paradise Lost:*

> Thou from the first
> Wast present, and with mighty wings outspread
> Dove-like satst *brooding* on the vast Abyss
> And mad'st it pregnant.
>
> (1.19–22; emphasis added)

Longinus observes that the idea of sublimity is most clearly seen in the account of creation given in the opening verses of Genesis.[6] So the Longinian, Miltonic, and Wordsworthian sublime as manifested in this watershed sonnet and its literary antecedents are in uneasy accord, Wordsworth's characteristic contribution being to give the mode a more personal, hence romantic, emphasis, involving as it does aqueous and admonitory (as well as confessional) elements expressed through powerful auditory imagery, with the whole cast in a patriarchal mold.

Wordsworth's greatest sonnet, "London, 1802," written in September of that year, likewise develops a double apocalyptic trope based on the aforementioned passage from Revelation. "Thy soul was like a Star" (9) echoes Saint John the Divine's vision of the returned Christ whose "countenance was as the sun shineth in his strength," and the comparison of Milton's voice to the roar of the ocean—"Thou hadst a voice whose sound was like the sea" (10)—once more recalls the antecedent verses from Revelation. This poem gains over the sonnet composed a month earlier on the beach at Calais by being given a more specific and clearly identified human focus: Milton is invoked as a type of Christ to return and (somewhat as in Blake's *Milton*) help to restore humankind to a condition of primal innocence. Although he at one point identifies himself with his degenerate countrymen for rhetorical purposes—"We are selfish men" (6)—Wordsworth really identifies with the poet-prophet Milton in his role as admonisher and sublime patriarchal example.

In his most daring sonnet, "The world is too much with us," Wordsworth again uses the sea as one of all his central images, this time humanized as a woman—"The Sea that bares her bosom to the moon" (5)—which *sounds* pagan; he also drops the auditory allusion to the passages from Revelation we have been discussing, or rather, subsumes their subtle and pervasive influence within the sound qualities of his verse, complete with sonorous long vowels doubtless showing the influence of Milton:

> Great God! I'd rather be
> A Pagan suckled in a creed outworn;
> So might I, standing on this pleasant lea,
> Have glimpses that would make me less forlorn;
> Have sight of Proteus rising from the sea;
> Or hear old Triton blow his wreathed horn.
>
> (9–14)

Whatever one might think of these waters, they are clearly not stagnant. The admonitory tone of the octave has given way to the radically apocalyptic one of the sestet, wherein the gods are heard as well as seen. It is perhaps no coincidence that, judging from its influence on his own work, this seems to have been Keats's favorite Wordsworthian sonnet.

Wordsworth's remarkable lyric now generally known as the "Immortality Ode," written roughly contemporaneously with the sonnets we have just been discussing, is a virtual palinode insofar as it recants a major portion of his nature-based philosophy: "But yet I know, where'er I go, / That there hath past away a glory from the earth" (17–18). The two long years it took Wordsworth to come up with a satisfactory explanation for this poignant sense of loss, and the evident sublimity of the result, testify not only to the brooding power of his intellect, but also, no doubt, to the effectiveness of Coleridge's Neoplatonic tutelage:

> Not in entire forgetfulness,
> And not in utter nakedness,
> But trailing clouds of glory do we come
> From God, who is our home:
>
> (62–65)

The fountain of light image implicit here, and explicit in a later line—"the fountain-light of all our day" (155)—is pure Plotinus, artfully synthesized with visionary Christianity, as the poem's biblical echoes attest.[7]

The pattern of aqueous and admonitory elements is evident not only in the etherealized "fountain-light" trope, which immediately follows an admonitory passage

> Blank misgivings of a Creature
> Moving about in worlds not realised,
> High instincts before which our mortal Nature
> Did tremble like a guilty Thing surprised:
>
> (148–51)

but also in the sequel (to be discussed presently), which concludes what is easily the longest stanza in the poem.

As the fountain-light image combines aspects of the passages from the first chapter of Revelation we have been discussing—the comparison of the returned Christ's face to the "sun [which] shineth in his strength" and his voice to "the sound of many waters"—each individual is now seen as a type of Christ:

> The Soul that rises with us, our life's Star,
> Hath had elsewhere its setting,
> And cometh from afar:
>
> (59–61)

One's progress from birth through life and death may thus be illuminated by the glow of the transcendent source that is also, by a splendid synaesthetic oxymoron, simultaneously seen and heard as a symbolic vision of the ultimate goal:

> Hence in a season of calm weather
> Though inland far we be,
> Our Souls have sight of that immortal sea
> Which brought us hither,
> Can in a moment travel thither,
> And *see* the Children sport upon the shore,
> And *hear* the mighty waters *rolling* evermore.
>
> (165–71; emphasis added)

However latently, we also *hear* the children and *see* the waters, rolled into one human and divine entity in which childhood and adulthood, as well as the imaginatively apprehended environment, are imaginatively combined. Insofar as children *qua* children are androgynous, Wordsworth may be said to have attained the androgynous sublime in this, his greatest single poem.

The echo of *Paradise Lost* (1.19–20) in an earlier passage addressing Hartley Coleridge as the prototypical child—

"Thou, over whom thy Immortality / *Broods* like the Day, a Master o'er a slave" (118–19; emphasis added)—shows Wordsworth successfully (*pace* Coleridge) fusing creation with recreation, Genesis with Revelation, and once more achieving the sublime, this time with patriarchal overtones. The tension between these two different modes of the sublime, the patriarchal and the androgynous, with the former usually dominating, is felt throughout Wordsworth's greatest poetry.

Apocalypse and the Death of Dad*

In book 1 of *The Prelude* it is the voice of the River Derwent whose "murmurs" and "ceaseless music" Wordsworth chiefly remembers (271–77). The retrospective account a few lines further on of the boy William standing alone beneath the sky

> as if I had been born
> On Indian plains, and from my mother's hut
> Had run abroad in wantonness, to sport
> A naked savage, in the thunder shower.
>
> (1.297–300)

invites comparison with lines 170–71 of the Immortality Ode insofar as it once more fuses auditory and visual imagery in a trope with apocalyptic overtones. "Thunder shower," with its low-keyed echo of Revelation, coming as it does after "wantonness" and "naked savage," recapitulates the aqueous and admonitory sublime.

In contrast, the "huge peak, black and huge" (378) that looms up over the lake as if to admonish William for taking an impromptu joy ride in the famous boat-stealing episode is almost entirely visual, as are the "huge and mighty forms" (398) that haunted him for several days and nights thereafter. But once more, aqueous and admonitory elements are significantly combined, albeit with a different emphasis.

The same is true of Wordsworth's purloined (from Descartes) dream in book 5 of the Arab phantom offering him a stone and a shell, the latter reminiscent of Apollo's (actually, Hermes') lyre (which was made from a tortoise shell) and prophesying "Destruction to the children of the earth / By deluge, now at hand" (97–98). The business of the drowned man who surfaces later in this book is in a similar vein. Wordsworth accepts the stone as well as the

---

dad n. (colloq., in oaths etc.) God [corrupt.] *(OED)*.

shell because his poetry has a proto-Einsteinian aspect: its awareness that mass is a form of energy, and its portrayals of ghosts (including that of the discharged veteran at the end of book 4) are usually pervaded by a self-accepting acquiescence, suggesting that the natural human being, of whom the specter is a symbol, while ultimately faced with destruction, is meanwhile playing a necessary part in the cosmic scheme of things.[8]

The most explicitly apocalyptic passage in *The Prelude* is of course the Simplon Pass episode in book 6. Wordsworth's experience of the French Revolution, signaled in the earlier description of Mont Blanc (523–28), finds its appropriate analogue in the lines—"Loth to believe what we so grieved to hear, / For still we had hopes that pointed to the clouds" (6.586–87)—which come just a few lines before the strangely anticlimactic realization *"that we had crossed the Alps"* (591). The theme of the passage immediately following this, as well as of *The Prelude* writ large, is that a revolution can be truly experienced only in the mind:

> Our destiny, our being's heart and home,
> Is with infinitude, and only there;
> With hope it is, hope that can never die,
> Effort, and expectation, and desire,
> And something evermore about to be.
> Under such banners militant, the soul
> Seeks for no trophies, struggles for no spoils
> That may attest her prowess, blest in thoughts
> That are their own perfection and reward,
> Strong in herself and in beatitude
> That hides her, like the mighty flood of Nile
> Poured from his fount of Abyssinian clouds
> To fertilize the whole Egyptian plain.
>
> (6.604–16)

The mind-river trope shows Wordsworth at his most magisterial, echoing James Bruce's *Travels to Discover the Source of the Nile* (1791), as well as Coleridge's unpublished "Kubla Khan," the latter of which likewise deals with the theme of human and divine creativity reinforcing one another in an exotic setting.

The following passage, in which Wordsworth describes his and his companion Robert Jones's descent into Gondo Gorge, brings the theme of apocalypse to a crescendo:

> the immeasurable height
> Of woods decaying, never to be decayed,

> The stationary blasts of waterfalls,
> And in the narrow rent at every turn
> Winds thwarting winds, bewildered and forlorn,
> The torrents shooting from the clear blue sky,
> The rocks that *muttered* close upon our ears,
> Black drizzling crags that *spake* by the way-side
> *As if a voice were in them,* the sick sight,
> And giddy prospect of the *raving* stream,
> The unfettered clouds and region of the Heavens,
> Tumult and peace, the darkness and the light—
> Were all like workings of one mind, the features
> Of the same face, blossoms upon one tree;
> Characters of the great Apocalypse,
> The types and symbols of Eternity,
> Of first, and last, and midst, and without end.
>   (6.624–40; emphasis added)

This famous passage once more echoes Saint John the Divine's vision of the returned Christ (as I have indicated by the use of italics): "his voice as the sound of many waters" (Rev. 1:15). There is of course fear as well as beauty in this passage ("the sick sight / And giddy prospect of the raving stream") but in addition to sounding the admonitory note Wordsworth is setting the reader up for his assertion toward the end of the poem that love and imagination ultimately transcend fear by resolving everything into the transformed (and implicitly androgynous) humanity of God (14. 188–205), a God in whom Wordsworth, during his most creative period, half believes and half disbelieves. Thomas Weiskel observes that line 638, quoted above, contains Wordsworth's only poetic use of the word *Apocalypse* and that he ends the passage by "aligning it conspicuously with Adam and Eve's morning hymn to the Creator, 'Him first, him last, him midst, and without end.'"[9] (Blake, interestingly enough, never uses the word.) Line 640 also again echoes Revelation (1:17): "I am the first and the last." In spite of the androgynous sound of some of these echoes, Wordsworth is symbolically standing alone with his Creator here, and the passage as a whole is cast in a patriarchal rather than an androgynous mold, pervaded by a peculiar stasis.

Curiously, in the lines immediately following this apocalyptic passage, Wordsworth refers to himself and Robert Jones in their lodging that night as having been almost overcome by the experience:

>   deafened and stunned
> By noise of waters, making innocent sleep

> Lie melancholy among weary bones.
>
> (6. 646–48)

In 1820 Wordsworth with his wife and sister revisited the "dreary mansion" where he and Jones had spent what Dorothy in her journal calls the "awful night" of thirty years earlier, and Wordsworth could not be persuaded to accompany her within.[10] Whatever the exact nature of the experience, no doubt it was traumatic: Wordsworth had learned that a vision of hell may well precede, and later be subsumed within, one of heaven. (One may contrast the dreary weather Wordsworth and Jones experienced while crossing the Alps with the paradisal day on which Byron and Hobhouse climbed the Lauberhorn, an experience Byron enthusiastically recorded in his journals, and one which is of course germane to *Manfred*.[11]) In 1790 Wordsworth simply did not possess the superstructure of Christian belief on which he was later able to build this climactic passage into its aesthetically satisfying, if existentially puzzling, shape.

The explanation for Wordsworth's trauma and sense of guilt is no doubt Freudian, as has been shown elsewhere.[12] This is most clearly seen in the "spots of time" passage from book 12 of *The Prelude*, where Wordsworth recalls two episodes from his boyhood. The first of these involves his self-identification with a murderer who "had been hung in iron chains" at a spot where someone had subsequently "carved the murderer's name" (236–40). The boy William's reaction upon seeing these letters cut in the turf is remarkable indeed:

> A casual glance had shown them, and I fled,
> Faltering and faint, and ignorant of the road:
> Then, reascending the bare common, saw
> A naked pool that lay beneath the hills,
> The beacon on the summit, and, more near,
> A girl who bore a pitcher on her head,
> And seemed with difficult steps to force her way
> Against the blowing wind. It was, in truth,
> An ordinary sight; but I should need
> Colours and words that are unknown to man,
> To paint the visionary dreariness
> Which, while I looked all round for my lost guide,
> Invested moorland waste, and naked pool,
> The beacon crowning the lone eminence,
> The female and her garments vexed and tossed
> By the strong wind.
>
> (12.246–61)

Here sex, as represented by the wind-whipped girl, at one point significantly called a "female," is associated with guilt, as symbolized by the murderer (said to have killed his wife) with whom the boy William identifies.

The second "of these memorials" concerns the death of Wordsworth's father, which took place during the Christmas break from school when he was thirteen (12.289–316). It seems pretty obvious that Wordsworth, unconsciously, or—I suspect—consciously, anticipated his father's death, which, when it happened, made him feel guilty. Hence he describes himself as having "bowed low / To God, Who thus corrected my desires" (12.315–16); that is, he accepted the guilt as a necessary chastisement or punishment for his pubescent oedipal longings.[13] Behind both passages is the oedipal pattern of rebellion against the father imago, as represented by the judicial and educational systems of the time.

Immediately following these passages is another vivid evocation of the aqueous and admonitory sublime:

> And, afterwards, the wind and sleety rain,
> And all the business of the elements,
> The single sheep, and the one blasted tree,
> And the bleak music from that old stone wall,
> *The noise of wood and water,* and the mist
> That on the line of each of those two roads
> Advanced in such *indisputable shapes;*
> All these were kindred spectacles and sounds
> To which I oft repaired; and *thence would drink,*
> *As at a fountain;*
>
> (12.317–26; emphasis added)

The single sheep, blasted tree, and stone wall are synecdochic reminders of a ruined paradise,[14] and the mist advancing along the two roads in "indisputable shapes" may be meant to recall Milton's portrayal of Sin and Death at the gates of hell in *Paradise Lost,* including Satan's description of Death as an "execrable shape" (2.681). Hence the admonitory note is once more sounded. The most remarkable aspect of the passage, however, is not Wordsworth's quasi-satanic self-portrayal, here as in the earlier "spectral" episodes, since these tend to fall in with the romantic revaluation of Milton's portrayal of Satan, but rather the degree of self-acceptance underlying the positive note on which the passage ends, with the water imagery no longer admonitory but sustaining and restorative, the fountain of life. It would seem that Wordsworth was adept at having the best of both worlds.

As in the earlier boat-stealing episode that serves as a paradigm for much of what follows in *The Prelude,* aspects of human personality that conventional morality might seek to ignore or rationalize away are recognized by Wordsworth as sources of energy waiting to be tapped and harnessed. Psychologically, Wordsworth may be said to have "killed off" his father, as he was later to "kill off" Dorothy and Coleridge, the better to arrogate to himself their psychic energy and power. (*Power* has long been recognized as a key word in Wordsworth's poetry.) Wordsworth's deepest desire was to become his own father and patriarch, the better to replace and paradoxically identify with the orthodox God with whom he was, throughout much of his life, consciously or unconsciously in contention. The poetic result is what I have termed the *patriarchal sublime,* which sustained Wordsworth until the death of his brother John, whom, unlike his parents and the others mentioned, Wordsworth saw as a surrogate for himself: "A power is gone which nothing can restore; / A deep distress hath humanized my soul" ("Elegiac Stanzas," 35–36).

From Darkness to Light

In book 13 of *The Prelude,* appropriately enough, Wordsworth describes himself bending "in reverence / To Nature" (223–24) and, after twice asking Coleridge's forgiveness in the 1805 text (a passage that was later omitted) he proposes that the poet may become "a power like one of Nature's" (312). This is immediately followed by a remarkable passage in which Wordsworth conjures up a vision of Druid human sacrifices on Salisbury Plain:

> I called on Darkness—but before the word
> Was uttered, midnight darkness seemed to take
> All objects from my sight; and lo! again
> The Desert visible by dismal flames;
> It is the sacrificial altar, fed
> With living men—how deep the groans! the voice
> Of those that crowd the giant wicker thrills
> The monumental hillocks, and the pomp
> Is for both worlds, the living and the dead.
>
> (13.327–35)

By "Darkness" Wordsworth presumably means the powers of Darkness, strained though the interpretation may seem to some. "Desert visible" echoes Milton's "Darkness Visible." This is one of Wordsworth's most explicit attempts at the satanic sublime.

Wordsworth crossed Salisbury Plain alone and on foot in late July or early August 1793 en route to Wales. He was without money or prospects, and had but recently abandoned Annette Vallon shortly before she was to give birth to their child. Wordsworth's spiritual dryness during this period may be symbolized by the fact that Salisbury Plain is inland and there are few streams about. At any rate, the aqueous and admonitory element is conspicuously lacking. The scene ends with a vision of Druid astronomers, which Blake would unhesitatingly have called Urizenic.

In marked contrast to this is the heavenly sublime of the Mount Snowdon passage with which *The Prelude* comes to its final crescendo. Once more the scene is at night, although this time Wordsworth is not alone but in (male) company, as he was when crossing the Alps. The imminent apocalyptic vision is signaled by the sudden apparition of the moon:

> For instantly a light upon the turf
> Fell like a flash, and lo! as I looked up,
> The Moon hung *naked* in a firmament
> Of azure without cloud, and at my feet
> Rested *a silent sea of hoary mist*.
> (14.38–42; emphasis added)

"Naked" is always an apocalyptic word in Wordsworth, and the moon, traditionally feminine, is here combined with potentially redemptive water imagery—"a silent sea of hoary mist"—in contrast to the spiritual and physical dessication of Salisbury Plain. That the sea of mist is silent at this point is emphasized by the atypical doubling of the image a few lines further on:

> only the inferior stars
> Had disappeared, or shed a fainter light
> In the clear presence of the full-orbed Moon,
> Who, from her sovereign elevation, gazed
> Upon *the billowing ocean, as it lay*
> *All meek and silent*.
> (14.51–56; emphasis added)

Wordsworth is here setting the reader up for the thunderous echo of Revelation that immediately follows:

> save that through a rift—
> Not distant from the shore whereon we stood,

> A fixed, abysmal, gloomy, breathing-place—
> *Mounted the roar of waters, torrents, streams*
> *Innumerable, roaring with one voice!*
> *Heard over earth and sea,* and, in that hour,
> For so it seemed, felt by the starry heavens.
>
> (14.56–62; emphasis added)

Although it may have had a natural basis, this is clearly no natural voice, as is suggested by the synaesthetic use of the word "vision" two lines further on: "When into air had partially dissolved / That vision" (14.63–64). Wordsworth goes on to say that the powerful auditory hallucination was a symbol of the Godhead, now oxymoronically alive:

> There I beheld the emblem of a mind
> That feeds upon infinity, that *broods*
> *Over the dark abyss,* intent to *hear*
> *Its voices issuing forth to silent light*
> *In one continuous stream.*
>
> (14.70–74; emphasis added)

Here synaesthesia once more becomes oxymoron, the contrary of Milton's "darkness visible," just as the "one voice" of the previous passage now becomes the plural "voices," suggesting an almost Blakean concept of divine unity-in-multiplicity, or marriage of heaven and hell, complete with sublime intimations of androgyny welling up from below.

Wordsworth goes on to postulate a Miltonic hierarchy of creative spirits, which are monads of the Godhead and in which all creation synecdochically participates:

> Such minds are truly from the Deity,
> For they are Powers; and hence the highest bliss
> That flesh can know is theirs—the consciousness
> Of whom they are, habitually infused
> Through every image and through every thought,
> And all affections by communion raised
> From earth to heaven, from human to divine.
>
> (14.112–18)

The "roar of waters" and "one continuous stream" passages that precede this one constitute Wordsworth's most effective (because most transcendent) use of the aqueous but no longer admonitory sublime. The darkness and light, sound and silence, as well as their

traditional gender equivalents, stand in reciprocal relations, each
implicitly enhancing the ineffable other.[15]

Wordsworth comes closest to abandoning the patriarchal for the
androgynous sublime in his Lucy poems, where he achieves true
at-one-ment with what Jung would call his anima, or the feminine
side of his nature. Whether the beautiful maiden portrayed in these
haunting lyrics is an idealized portrait of Dorothy—whom Wordsworth was about to "abandon" in favor of matrimony—or is entirely a creature of his imagination perhaps doesn't matter very
much. In these poems alone Wordsworth sounds authentic as a
love poet, attaining an androgynous sublimity that is lacking in
some of his more famous poems. Lucy, whose name may derive
from the Latin *lux,* meaning light, is androgynous in the sense that
she remains childlike or virginal, albeit loved, both by a maternal
presence called "Nature" and by the speaker. The latter, in addition
to having enjoyed the imaginative androgyny of being a lover (the
lover qua lover is androgynous) also experiences the humanizing
androgyny of grief: "But she is in her grave, and oh, / The difference to me!" ("She dwelt among the untrodden ways," 11–12).
   Frances Ferguson has shown how Wordsworth in *The Excursion*
sometimes "calls all poetry into question as a possibly spurious
sublimity," belatedly rebelling against the self-entrapment of what
Keats was to diagnose as "the wordsworthian or egotistical sublime."[16] But this gesture was partially implicit in the Lucy poems
with their valorization of a quiet, modest, shy but loving life, however brief, when measured against a "poetic" but sometimes selfish
and obtuse one. Once more, sublimity transcending reason is seen
as inseparable from imaginative androgyny.[17]
   Geoffrey Hartman, in his interesting discussion of the Lucy
poems, stops just short of calling them sublime, on the ground that
"the strange and familiar, the (German) sublime and the (English)
pathos are mixed so evenly."[18] But it is just such a mixture that
we have seen to constitute the androgynous sublime, as Blake intimates toward the end of *Jerusalem:*

> no more the Masculine mingles
> With the Feminine but the Sublime is shut out from the Pathos
> In howling torment, to build stone walls of separation. .
> (*J* 90:10–12)

With the partial exception of Lucy, Wordsworth's solitaries are
just that—solitary, with little or no social or sexual interaction.

Among the few other apparent exceptions are the old couple in "Michael," who really prove the rule by being cast in a patriarchal mold that makes effective communication and child-rearing difficult if not impossible, in spite of Michael's stressed nursing of Luke, which seems rather more possessive than otherwise. Luke is never consulted about his father's disastrous plan to send him to London to save the family farm: he is merely expected to shut up and obey, which makes his eventual rebellion come as something of a (probably unintended) psychic release for the reader. The patriarchal sublime has collapsed into the patriarchal mock pathos.

It may be concluded that Wordsworth—to put the matter in convenient Blakean terms—remained the poetical Urizen among the major romantics in the sense that, with such rare and beautiful exceptions as those noted, he did not succeed in fully incorporating the feminine side of his nature, or what Blake would have called his emanation, into his vision, preferring instead to retain a hard core of masculine identity.

3

Coleridge: From the Analogical to the Androgynous Sublime

The Spiritual Sun and the Divine Analogue

COLERIDGE'S CONCEPT OF THE SUBLIME FIRST EMERGES IN HIS early sonnet "Pantisocracy" (1794), the name of the ideal society he and a group of friends hoped to establish on the banks of the Susquehanna River in Pennsylvania. The poem reflects Coleridge's hopes for his own poetic development based on the burgeoning cult of the poetic genius:

> Sublime of Hope, I seek the cottag'd dell
> Where Virtue calm with careless step may stray,
> And dancing to the moonlight roundelay,
> The wizard Passions weave an holy spell.
>
> (5–8)

To the twenty-two-year-old Coleridge's youthful use of the "hopeful sublime" (which he may be deliberately contrasting to Burke's fearful sublime) is added his characteristic image of the spiritual sun, as he proposes to "see the rising Sun, and feel it dart / New rays of pleasance trembling to the heart" (13–14).

The same image recurs in Coleridge's second sonnet on Pantisocracy, wherein he proposes to banish despots with "the immortal mind's expanding ray / Of everlasting Truth" (7–8), and again in his sonnet to the imprisoned "La Fayette," which concludes: "For lo! the Morning struggles into Day, / And Slavery's spectres shriek and vanish from the ray!"

The image of the spiritual sun, which becomes something of a leitmotif in Coleridge's poetry of this period (1794–95), is meant to herald the dawn of universal regeneration, somewhat as in Blake's roughly contemporaneous "A Song of Liberty," both poets' imaginations having been set ablaze by sparks wafting across the channel from the incipient inferno in France.

This theme may be seen writ large in Coleridge's uneven poem "Religious Musings" (1794), which combines revolutionary fervor with millennial expectations. The image of the spiritual sun predominates, as in an epic simile supposedly describing the regeneration of the Elect through faith:

> As when a shepherd on a vernal morn
> Through some thick fog creeps timorous with slow foot,
> Darkling he fixes on the immediate road
> His downward eye: all else of fairest kind
> Hid or deformed. But lo! the bursting Sun!
>
> (94–98)

Coleridge's note to this passage explains, "Our evil Passions, under the influence of Religion, become innocent, and may be made to animate our virtue—in the same manner as the thick mist melted by the Sun, increases the light which it had before excluded."[1]

This is followed a few lines further on by an indication of the rhetorical context in which the previous passage, if not the whole poem, is conceived:

> There is one Mind, one omnipresent Mind,
> Omnific. His most holy name is Love.
> Truth of subliming import!
>
> (105–7)

The poem ends with a "sublime" passage in which reference to Leibnitz's doctrine of monads (i.e., the divine analogue: we are all participants in God's creativity[2]) is combined once more with the image of the spiritual sun:

> Contemplant Spirits! ye that hover o'er
> With untired gaze the immeasurable fount
> Ebullient with creative Deity!
> And ye of plastic power, that interfused
> Roll through the grosser and material mass
> In organizing surge! Holies of God!
> (And what if Monads of the infinite mind?) . . .
> Soaring aloft I breathe the empyreal air
> Of Love, omnific, omnipresent Love,
> Whose day-spring rises glorious in my soul
> As the great Sun, when he his influence

> Sheds on the frost-bound waters—The glad stream
> Flows to the ray and warbles as it flows.
>
> (402–19)

The self-reflexive onomatopoetic use of the aqueous sublime in the last line-and-a-half anticipates, and may have influenced, that of Wordsworth.

Sometimes Coleridge's poetry of this period has a more inward-looking quality, which gives rise to a more authentic sublime. In the sonnet "To Rev. W. L. Bowles," the theme of the divine analogue (what Coleridge elsewhere calls the imagination as "a dim Analogue of . . . all that we can *conceive* of creation"[3]) emerges,

> Bidding a strange mysterious PLEASURE brood
> Over the wavy and tumultuous mind,
> As the great SPIRIT erst with plastic sweep
> Mov'd on the darkness of the unform'd deep.
>
> (Second version; 11–14)

These twin images of what I have called the spiritual sun and the divine analogue are really one: the former relates nature to divinity, while the latter dovetails human and divine creativity. Both are central to Coleridge's developing sense of sublimity.

The "strange mysterious PLEASURE," which implicitly symbolizes what Coleridge was later to call the Imagination, both primary and secondary, broods over the unconscious mind as the Spirit of God moved (or brooded) lovingly and mysteriously over the waters in the Genesis and Miltonic accounts of creation. The words "plastic" and "unform'd" also suggest a Neoplatonic influence, as well as a Platonic one emanating from the formative role of the demiurge in the *Timaeus*. The lines, amazingly rich and compact in their allusiveness, may be represented by a diagram:

Genesis	**Plotinus**	**Coleridge**
The Spirit of God	*One*	*Pleasure*
⋀	⋀	⋀
The Waters	*Nous*	*The Unconscious Mind*

Each of these is of course a paradigm of the others.

The concept of the analogical sublime recurs with a difference in some speculative lines from "The Eolian Harp," Coleridge's protohoneymoon poem composed at Clevedon, Somersetshire, in the summer of 1795:

> And what if all of animated nature
> Be but organic Harps diversely fram'd,
> That tremble into thought, as o'er them sweeps
> Plastic and vast, one intellectual breeze,
> At once the Soul of each, and God of all?
>
> (44–48)

The tentative tone of this, as contrasted with the ending of the sonnet to Bowles, no doubt has to do with the conversational mode of the poem and Coleridge's inner uncertainties about his new relationship with Sara—a defect, if it is one, that Coleridge attempted to remedy with some more assertive lines added in 1817:

> O! the one Life within us and abroad,
> Which meets all motion and becomes its soul,
> A light in sound, a sound-like power in light,
> Rhythm in all thought, and joyance every where—
>
> (26–29)

The graceful synaesthesia of line 28, reflecting no doubt the older Coleridge's investigations into the nature of sound, is followed by a wonderfully succinct statement of the pulsating, transcendental source of life as a divine nexus of thought and feeling, in which the earlier emphasis on the pleasure principle becomes a veritable dance of creation.

Another aspect of the analogical sublime in Coleridge's early verse is his emphasis on the theme of self-transcendence in and through direct experience of nature, in a manner anticipating Wordsworth as well as the later romantics. Thus his climb up the steep and stony mount in "Reflections on Having Left a Place of Retirement," meant to be on one level an allegory of the ascent of Parnassus, culminates in an expression of feelings of the close conjunction of heaven and earth. The typically Coleridgean double emphasis on the bleakness of the mountain—"*Here* the bleak mount, / The bare bleak mountain" (29–30)—is meant to suggest a contrast between what Spinoza calls the *natura naturata* (mere nature) and the *natura naturans* (nature naturing), the latter being a closer approximation to the Godhead:

> The Channel *there*, the Islands and white sails,
> Dim coasts, the cloud-like hills, and shoreless Ocean—

> It seem'd like Omnipresence! God, methought,
> Had built him there a Temple: the whole World
> Seem'd *imag'd* in its vast circumference:
> No *wish* profan'd my overwhelmed heart.
> Blest hour! It was a luxury,—to be!
>
> (36–42)

The following line, not too surprisingly, contains the exclamation "Mount Sublime!" thus indicating the rhetorical context in which the apocalyptic moment of this poem is meant to be seen. Each of Coleridge's half-dozen or so conversation poems, a genre he virtually invented, builds up to such an apocalyptic moment.

One of the best of these poems is "This Lime-Tree Bower My Prison," written at Nether Stowey in July 1797, on the cusp of Coleridge's miraculous year. Here the apocalyptic moment is characteristically experienced, at least hypothetically, by both the poet and his "gentle-hearted Charles [Lamb]," or double:

> So my friend
> Struck with deep joy may stand as I have stood,
> Silent with swimming sense; yea, gazing round
> On the wide landscape, gaze till all doth seem
> Less gross than bodily . . .
>
> (37–41)

Thus a sort of mystic communion of both friends and "the Almighty Spirit, when yet he makes / Spirits perceive his presence" (42–43) is attained.

One notices the progression toward a tone of greater certitude and exactness in the phrasing here, as contrasted to the earlier conversation poems. One may ask, what does Coleridge mean by "swimming sense" and "less gross than bodily"? The former phrase anticipates the eddying or going forth and returning of the senses to create the environment that is referred to in the last stanza of "Dejection: an Ode" (135–36), and the latter one Wordsworth's "we are laid asleep / In body, and become a living soul" ("Tintern Abbey," 46–47), with its somewhat dualistic, hence inferior, emphasis. As someone has remarked, vision is the thawing of the body.[4]

Lines 42–43, previously quoted in part, suggest revelation of absolute form perceived behind the changing phenomena of nature, although the Almighty Spirit is still said to be "veiled." Unlike the later Shelley, Coleridge does not want to tear aside the veil of nature, being content with the intimation of immortality that the transcendent moment offers. The various hues that "veil the Al-

mighty Spirit" are meant to suggest that nature is God's double.[5]
It is first viewed with revulsion in the form of the "dark green file
of long lank weeds" (17)—adder's tongue ferns, as Coleridge's note
informs us—anticipating the Mariner's first sight of the water
snakes in "The Rime of the Ancient Mariner." Just as the Mariner
later blesses the water snakes, Coleridge, after the apocalyptic
moment has passed, blesses the "last rook" (68) of evening, whose
purple plumage as it crosses the setting sun—a submerged but
important color motif—was anticipated by the earlier reference to
"purple shadow" (26) and "purple heath flowers" (35). Coleridge is
once more anticipating the apocalyptic moment when the Mariner
blesses the water snakes:

> blue, glossy green, and velvet black,
> They coiled and swam; and every track
> Was a flash of golden fire.
>
> (278–80)

Coleridge is saying we cannot apprehend God directly, but only
indirectly, through his creatures, which is why he preferred the
sublime surrogate moon to the patristic, theistic sun:

> The moving Moon went up the sky,
> And no where did abide:
> Softly she was going up,
> And a star or two beside—
>
> (263–67)

As the gloss wonderfully puts it, "In his loneliness and fixedness
[the Mariner] yearneth towards the journeying Moon, and the stars
that still sojourn, yet still move onward; and every where the blue
sky belongs to them, and is their appointed rest, and their native
country and their own natural homes, which they enter unan-
nounced, as lords that are certainly expected and yet there is a
silent joy at their arrival." This sublime passage immediately pre-
cedes the Mariner's blessing of the water snakes, which is of
course the emotional climax as well as the turning point of the
poem.

The moon "veils" the sun by reflecting its light, which helps to
make it an apt symbol of divine (as well as sublime) androgyny:

> Still as a slave before his lord,
> The ocean hath no blast;

> His great bright eye most silently
> Up to the Moon is case—
>
> If he may know which way to go;
> For she guides him smooth or grim.
> See, brother, see! how graciously
> She looketh down on him.
>
> (413–21)

Here the moon is described as by turns lordlike and feminine. The mode and motif of sublime androgyny is doubled in the earlier description of the (male) spirit's voice that speaks the passage just quoted: "The other was a softer voice, / As soft as honey-dew" (406–7).

The moon, which Robert Penn Warren argues is a symbol of Imagination, is—somewhat like the portrayal of the sun—also ambivalent, signifying the softer, feminine aspect of divine reality beneath which the Mariner can begin to work out his redemption.[6] Her double or spectre is the "Nightmare life-in-death" who chills men's blood and claims the Mariner as her prize. The artful ambivalence of her portrayal—not "death-in-life," but "life-in-death"—also suggests an element of redemptive vitalism. The two faces of the moon are different aspects of what certain eighteenth-century mythographers called "the Great Mother of the Gods," variously identified with the Greek Demeter, Rhea-Cybele, and Selene. In thus emphasizing the role of the redemptive, feminine moon as contrasted to the wrathful, patristic sun, Coleridge is anticipating the proto-feminism and androgyny of certain passages in Blake's *Jerusalem* and Shelley's *Prometheus Unbound*. The androgynous sublime thus once more becomes an important, albeit hitherto neglected, mode and motif of English romantic poetry.

Coleridge's Androgynous Sublime

The locus classicus of this mode is Coleridge's much maligned and misunderstood "Christabel." In a recent study of friendships among English romantic poets, I suggested that "Christabel" is Coleridge's attempt to "transform Wordsworth"; that is, to portray a creative metamorphosis of their relationship in which its spiritual essence would be simultaneously revealed and concealed. Coleridge would have agreed with Blake that the best art "is not too Explicit . . . because it rouzes the faculties to act." He also would have agreed with Blake's observation that "Without Minute Neatness of Execution The Sublime cannot Exist! Grandeur of Ideas is founded on Precision of Ideas."[7] The sublime is of course essentially a mode rather than a set of concepts, and the manner and style of "Christabel"—that poet's poem—have fascinated readers from Byron on (Byron called it "a wild and singularly original and beautiful poem"[8]). Both Byron ad Scott had heard "Christabel" recited, and both cribbed its meter before it was finally published in 1816 through Byron's generous influence some nineteen years after its inception.

In his preface to "Christabel" Coleridge says that it is "founded on a new principle: namely, that of counting in each line the accents, not the syllables. Though the latter may vary from seven to twelve, yet in each line the accents will be found to be only four." With all due respect to Coleridge, one cannot help but note that in line 3—which admittedly consists of only the hooting of an owl—there are not seven syllables but four, as there are in lines 57 and 264. Various critics have disputed Coleridge's claim to have discovered a "new principle" of versification in the poem. Nevertheless it must have *seemed* new to Byron and Scott, as well as to Wordsworth, all of whom imitated it with varying degrees of success, usually without acknowledgment.[9]

Perhaps what made the difference was Coleridge's handling of the meter, hinted at in the last line of the preface: "Nevertheless, this occasional variation in number of syllables is not introduced wantonly, or for the mere ends of convenience, but in correspondence with some transition in the nature of the imagery or passion." Thus in the two opening lines the verse begins quickly with twelve and eleven syllables respectively, and then slows down, as it were portentous of imminent disaster:

> 'Tis the middle of the night by the castle clock,
> And the owls have awakened the crowning cock;
> Tu-whit!—Tu-whoo!
> And hark, again! the crowing cock,
> How drowsily it crew.

> (1–5)

A similar effect is achieved by the typically Coleridgean device of doubling with a difference, or variegated repetition, combined with imagery suggestive of a discrepancy between appearance and reality:

> In the night chilly and dark?
> The night is chilly, but not dark

> The thin gray cloud is spread on high,
> It covers but not hides the sky.
> The moon is behind, and at the full;
> And yet she looks both small and dull.
>
> (14–19)

Another aspect of the style of "Christabel" that has received surprisingly little attention is Coleridge's skilful use of alliteration and assonance, which typically makes the line fall into two roughly equal halves, emphasizing the caesura. The binary effect is rather like that of Old English poetry, with the addition of rhyme:

And har*k*, again!   the *c*rowing *c*ock (4)

A *s*nake's *s*mall eye   blink*s* dull and *sh*y (583)

And with so*m*ewhat of *m*alice,   and *m*ore of dread (586)

In short, Coleridge seems to have anticipated not only Gerard Manley Hopkins's "sprung rhythm," with his idea of counting the accents instead of the syllables, but also Hopkins's adaptation of Old English alliteration. The result of all this—the binary line combined with syllabic variation in length and contrapuntal alliteration modulating the effect of the rhyme—is a supple, androgynous style that not only (as will be shown) echoes the sense, but also subverts conventional notions of sublimity while introducing new ones.

A fine, wild poem about a devout maid and a demon, "Christabel" begins at the witching hour in a forest outside a castle. Why is Christabel praying, not in her chamber or in the castle chapel, but "a furlong from the castle gate" beneath a huge oak tree covered with "moss and rarest misletoe" (26–35), all Druid plant fetishes? The answer would seem to be that Christabel, for all her exemplary piety, is unconsciously seeking out what she in fact finds "On the other side [i.e., beyond the threshold] . . . / Of the huge, broad-breasted, old oak tree" (41–42), namely the vampire witch Geraldine with her trumped-up tale of abduction who, once invited into Christabel's chamber and carried "[o]ver the threshold of the gate" (132), proceeds to psychically ravish her.[10]

Now I have argued at length elsewhere that this is on one level an allegory of Coleridge's "ravishment" by the psychically dominant Wordsworth, whose nature-based philosophy had made severe inroads into Coleridge's Christianized Neoplatonism.[11] Hence, Coleridge's perception of Wordsworth's "uncentering" influence, and his lifelong struggle to establish his own separate identity. To cite but one example: in "Fears in Solitude" (1798), written in a kind of quasi-Wordsworthian blank verse, Coleridge begins (and ends) the poem with some promising imagery of green light and golden furze, but the long middle portion sags like a limp soufflé with such uncharacteristic (for Coleridge) lines as the following:

> O native Britain! O my Mother Isle!
> How shouldst thou prove aught else but dear and holy
> To me, who from thy lakes and mountain-hills,
> Thy clouds, thy quiet dales, thy rocks and seas,
> Have drunk in all my intellectual life,
> All sweet sensations, all ennobling thoughts,
> All adoration of the God in nature?
>
> (182–88)

This embarrassing mock-Wordsworthian mode anticipates the more blatant and overt plagiarism (of another poet) and mock sublime of Coleridge's "Hymn Before Sunrise in the Vale of Chamouni" (1802), by which time Coleridge's partially self-willed destruction as a poet was all but complete.

As against this sort of thing, consider the imaginative precision of the following:

> A star hath set, a star hath risen,
> O Geraldine! since arms of thine
> Have been the lovely lady's prison.
> O Geraldine! one hour was thine—
> Thou'st had thy will! by tairn and rill,
> The night-birds all that hour were still.
> But now they are jubilant anew,
> From cliff and tower, tu-whoo! tu-whoo!
> Tu-whoo! tu-whoo! from wood and fell!
>
> (302–10)

The psychic transference and quasi-homosexual rape has taken place, and the nature of things is unalterably changed.

The next morning Christabel, who scarcely knows what has transpired, feels somehow sinful—"'Sure I have sinned!' said Christabel" (381)—and can but passively imitate her seducer. Christabel's plight is unforgettably emblematized by the image of a dove caught in the coils of a bright green snake:

> Green as the herbs on which it couched,
> Close by the dove's its head it crouched;
> And with the dove it heaves and stirs,
> Swelling its neck as she swelled hers!
>
> (551–53)

What, it may be asked, does all this have to do with androgyny? Chiefly, that by employing an artful translation of gender for his protagonist and antagonist in this *romance à clef,* Coleridge succeeded in making his most sublime poem almost critic-proof.[12] Whether or not one accepts the interpretation whose outline I have sketched—one which, it goes without saying, would have resonated with the depths of Coleridge's being and also has the advantage of explaining Wordsworth's vicious hostility to the poem, which (the poem, not the hostility) he tried to suppress—it seems evident that Christabel is a type of spiritual transformer embodying the concept of vicarious imaginative atonement, insofar as she suffers not for her absent lover, but for Geraldine: a psychic death she has unconsciously willed as surely as her prototype the infant Saint Teresa consciously (though ineffectually) sought martyrdom at the hands of the Moors.[13] Similarly, the androgynous sublime coupled with the divine analogue is manifested in Christabel's imitation of Christ as willing victim and vicarious atoner. The miracle of "Christabel" is thus that the subtlety of execution is very nearly equal to that of the concept, granted that the last thirty-four years of Coleridge's life constitute the third part of a tragic triptych, which he once referred to as "the song of [Christabel's] desolation."[14]

The mode of the androgynous sublime as manifested in "Christabel" also inferentially includes Dorothy Wordsworth, upon whom the character of Christabel seems partly modeled. Dorothy is almost certainly one of the prototypes for the "most gentle Maid" portrayed in the latter part of Coleridge's "The Nightingale," a conversation poem in which he addresses William and Dorothy at one point as "My Friend, and thou, our Sister!" (40). Somewhat like Christabel, the "most gentle Maid" dwells near a castle, is described as "hospitable" (69–70), and is in the habit of wandering about in the woods late at night communing (in what *is* a characteristic Coleridgean phrase) with "something more than Nature in the grove" (73). "The Nightingale" may thus be seen as either an imaginative adjunct to, or a partial recapitulation of, the mode of the androgynous sublime writ large in the transcendental transvestitism of "Christabel."

This mode, as distinct from its more flamboyant phallic counterpart, is discussed in all but name by Susan Luther in a perceptive article on "The Nightingale" wherein she remarks: "Coleridge's refusal to assume the role of epic or 'great' poet implies an alternate, equally viable aesthetic of modesty based upon self-sacrificing service to the Muse: the diffident poet's authority depends, not upon sublime self-assertion, but upon self-subordination."[15] As Blake put the matter in a different context, "The most sublime act is to set another before you."[16] What Coleridge is setting before himself in "The Nightingale" is not Wordsworth, and certainly not the admired Milton of "Il Penseroso," who is in fact somewhat heretically referred to in the poem, but rather the communal experience of "something more than Nature" he has just shared with William and Dorothy. The sometimes neglected importance of the latter is prophetically highlighted by the aforementioned passage concerning the "most gentle Maid," wherein the poem attains its quasi-fictive apotheosis. The emphasis on femininity is counterbalanced by the bird, who, as Luther observes, is "a joyous male who may be taken as a figure for the poetic nature-lover himself." Luther also usefully refers to the poem's "aesthetic of surrender, of self-sacrifice, humility, and renunciation of what might be called 'logocentric' control."[17] This idea is most clearly stated in a passage answering Milton's conceit of the melancholy bird and anticipating Keats's idea of negative capability:

> Poet who hath been building up the rhyme
> When he had better far have stretched his limbs
> Beside a brook in mossy forest-dell,
> By sun or moon-light, to the influxes
> Of shapes and sounds and shifting elements
> Surrendering his whole spirit, of his song
> And of his fame forgetful!
>
> (24–30)

The poem ends with Coleridge's "father's tale," wherein he himself as narrator and partial subject assumes a somewhat androgynous role in relation to his infant son Hartley, whom he nurses both physically and psychologically, perhaps overprotectively, but above all, unforgettably.

This motif of parental androgyny is seen most clearly in Coleridge's "Frost at Midnight," written in February 1798 during an interval in his composition of "The Ancient Mariner," and two months before "The Nightingale." The poem begins on a note of quiet sublimity: "The Frost performs its secret ministry / Unhelped by any wind." Using the "secret ministry" of frost as a metaphor for experience, Coleridge goes on to portray Hartley, the "Dear Babe" sleeping cradled by his side, as well as the wintry landscape outside his cottage. After referring to his own childhood at Christ's

Hospital school in London, he goes on to express the hope that Hartley may come to enjoy the beauty in nature that has been denied his father. Significantly unmentioned in the poem is Sara, Hartley's mother, who was presumably sleeping in another room, pregnant with her and Coleridge's second child. So in addition to using Hartley as a sort of alter ego, Coleridge is also assuming the roles of both father and mother, thus compounding the double motif with that of androgyny. These motifs are combined with that of cross-dressing in the retrospective lines, "Townsman, or aunt, or sister more beloved, / My play-mate when we both were clothed alike!" (42–3)[18] Thus the androgynous parent becomes once more the androgynous child.

The poem ends, as it began, on a note of quiet, almost unearthly sublimity:

> whether the eave-drops fall
> Heard only in the trances of the blast,
> Or if the secret ministry of frost
> Shall hang them up in silent icicles,
> Quietly shining to the quiet Moon.
>
> (70–74)

Here the ovoid eave-drops about to become icicles mirroring the moon—as if Coleridge and Hartley were both destined to freeze into a kind of forced maturity—may subliminally recall part of Plato's myth of the original androgyne:

> Now the sexes were three, and such as I have described them; because the sun, moon, and earth are three; and the man was originally the child of the sun, the woman of the earth, and the man-woman of the moon, which is made up of the sun and the earth, and they were all round and moved round and round like their parents.[19]

The connection of the moon with androgyny is, as we have seen, delicately adumbrated in *The Ancient Mariner* in the passage beginning

> 'Still as a slave before his lord,
> The ocean hath no blast;
> His great bright eye most silently
> Up to the Moon is cast.'
>
> (413–16)

What I have somewhat playfully referred to as the transcendental transvestitism of "Christabel" is also evident to a degree in

"Dejection: an Ode," Coleridge's swan song as a major poet. First addressed in the form of a verse-letter to Sara Hutchinson, then to "Wordsworth," then to "Edmund," and finally by a kind of quasi-androgynous compromise simply to "Lady," the poem deals with two related themes: Coleridge's death as a poet, and his psychological-cum-ontological quarrel with Wordsworth.

The poem's central image, "the new Moon / With the old Moon in her arms," from "The Ballad of Sir Patrick Spence," recapitulates the psychic symbiosis underlying "Christabel." Counterbalancing this double "feminine" image is the doubly fierce masculinity of the Wind, portrayed in stanza 7 as "Thou Actor, perfect in all tragic sounds!" reminiscent of the virile Edmund Kean, and also as "Thou mighty Poet, e'en to frenzy bold!" (108–9). Both images hark back to what Weiskel has called the phallic sublime. This motif, however, is in turn counterbalanced and softened later in the same stanza by the double feminine image of the "little child" who is lost, "And now moans low in bitter grief and fear, / And now screams loud, and hopes to make her mother hear." (124–25)

Nature is portrayed as feminine in the poem's central stanza, as the bride of the soul, another double motif that once more combines male with female elements:[20]

> O Lady! we receive but what we give
> And in our life alone does Nature live:
> Ours is her wedding garment, ours her shroud!
>   And would we aught behold, of higher worth,
> Than that inanimate cold world allowed
> To the poor loveless ever-anxious crowd,
>   Ah! from the soul itself must issue forth
> A light, a glory, a fair luminous cloud
>   Enveloping the Earth—
> And from the soul it self must there be sent
>   A sweet and potent voice, of its own birth,
> Of all sweet sounds the life and element!

(47–58)

Nature (feminine) is contained by the "wedding garment" (or "shroud") of the soul, which, insofar as the poet is masculine, *may* be implicitly masculine;[21] but the image of the envelope is once more feminine in the biological or sexual sense. The soul is not, strictly speaking, "wedding" nature, but only providing the vesture for a sacramental union that Coleridge would no doubt have seen in a mystical Christian context, rather reminiscent of the subtle androgynous vision underlying Blake's "To Spring."

At the end of this poem Coleridge is like a runner about to fall down and passing the torch on to someone else, whether "Sara," "Wordsworth," "Lady," or the reader. This motif of vicarious atonement or fulfilment is one of Coleridge's most characteristic gestures, undergirding as it does each of his three great poems. Even what has latterly been called the phallic sublime of "Kubla Khan" is undercut and to a degree made androgynous by the inspired poet's gesture of near despair towards the end, and of explicit dependence on the Abyssinian maid's "symphony and song" to revive within him his shared vision of heaven on earth, which he offers to pass on to the perceptive reader.

Coleridge's "Hymn Before Sunrise in the Vale of Chamouni" is, as aforementioned, an example of the mock sublime. Whatever might be said against the poem, it must be conceded that at least Coleridge avoids the aesthetic problem stated by Wordsworth in *The Prelude* apropos of his first sight of Mont Blanc:

> That very day,
> From a bare ridge we also first beheld
> Unveiled the summit of Mont Blanc, and grieved
> To have a soulless image on the eye
> That had usurped upon a living thought
> That never more could be
>
> (6.523–28)

That is to say, he avoids the problem by the simple expedient of never having been at Chamouni or having seen Mont Blanc except in his "mind's eye," which may be the whole point of the poem.

Northrop Frye has reminded us with a trenchant half-truth that poems are made out of other poems; Coleridge's grand larceny in transforming a poem of some twenty lines by Frederike Brun into a better one of some eighty lines, complete with partially pilfered preface, is at least in keeping with his doctrine that just as an idea can only be expressed by a symbol, so too we can achieve self-realization, of which the sublime is an important aspect, only through one another, "lending our minds out," as Browning's Fra Lippo Lippi put it.

Coleridge's semiplagiarized "Hymn" is not, on the whole, successful, partly because the multiple iteration of "God" in answer to a series of questions towards the end seems bullying and pedantic, if not patriarchal. Nevertheless, the poem influenced not only Shelley's early, uneven "Mont Blanc," but also Francis Thomp-

son's "Ode to the Setting Sun," the latter of which employs a similar though subtly different rhetorical technique closer to that of
Blake, at one point portraying the sun as androgynous:

> Thou twi-form deity, nurse at once and sire!
> Thou genitor that all things nourishest!
> The earth was suckled at thy shining breast
> And in her veins is quick thy milky fire.[22]

Perhaps Thompson was thinking of the ovoid shape of the sun and
Plato's myth of the androgyne. At any rate, he here makes explicit
the sublime androgyny that is implicit not only in Coleridge's curious "Hymn," with its bisexual authorship, but also Blake's "The
Tyger," which simply would not work without its antithetical or
"feminine" sublime in the penultimate stanza about the weeping
stars and the creation of the Lamb.[23]

The words *sublime* and *sublimity* are conspicuously—one is
tempted to say, mercifully—absent from Coleridge's "Hymn." The
former word, as well as something of its underlying reality, appears
in a late poem entitled "Limbo"; the word *limbo* comes from the
same root as, although its meaning is at the opposite remove from,
sublime. In this remarkable poem, which Coleridge wrote in 1817
(although it was not published until many years after his death),
he confronts head-on the psychic malaise that extended over the
last thirty-four years of his life:

> 'Tis a strange place, this Limbo!—not a Place,
> Yet name it so;—where Time and weary Space
> Fettered from flight, with night-mare sense of fleeing,
> Strive for their last crepuscular half-being;—
> Lank Space, and scytheless Time with branny hands
> Barren and soundless as the measuring sands,
> Nor mask'd by flit of Shades,—unmeaning they
> As moonlight on the dial of the day!
> But that is lovely—looks like Human Time,—
> An Old Man with a steady look sublime.
>
> (11–20)

This is closer to the mode of the French symbolists than that of
the romantics, which is to say ahead of its time; it also reminds
one of Blake, who likewise distinguishes between two different
forms of Time in his commentary on his lost painting, "A Vision
of the Last Judgment":

The Greeks represented Chronos or Time as a very Aged Man; this is Fable, but the Real Vision of Time is in Eternal Youth. I have, however, somewhat accommodated my Figure of Time to the common opinion, as I myself am also infected with it & my Visions also infected, as I see Time Aged, alas, too much so. (*K*, 614)

In Blake's myth Time and Space become his characters Los and Enitharmon:

> Los is by mortals nam'd Time, Enitharmon is nam'd Space
> But they [i.e., conventional artists] depict him bald & aged who
> is in eternal youth
> All powerful and his locks flourish like the brows of morning
> He is the Spirit of Prophecy the ever apparent Elias
>
> (*Mil* 24: 68–71)

Coleridge, who did not meet Blake until several years after "Limbo" was written, also accommodates his vision of Time to what Blake calls "borrowed opinion," but like him makes it new, both poets doubtless reflecting their own advancing age in their respective remarks. (Blake issued "A Vision of the Last Judgment" in 1810, when he was fifty-three; Coleridge was forty-five, but probably felt older, when he wrote "Limbo.") Blake also portrays Time as a (balding) old man in his illustrations to Edward Young's *Night Thoughts* (1797); but there he playfully endows Time with a single prominent forelock, to be seized by the alert beholder.

There is no doubt considerable self-portraiture in Coleridge's description of "Human Time" as a blind old man in "Limbo":

> An Old Man with a steady look sublime,
> That stops his earthly task to watch the skies;
> But he is blind—a Statue hath such eyes;—
> Yet having moonward turn'd his face by chance,
> Gazes the orb with moon-like countenance
> With scant white hairs, with foretop bald and high,
> He gazes still,—his eyeless face all eye,—
> As 'twere an organ full of silent sight,
> His whole face seemeth to rejoice in light!
> Lip touching lip, all moveless, bust and limb—
> He seems to gaze at that which seems to gaze on him!
>
> (20–30)

Unlike Blake's earlier illustrations to Young, some of which Coleridge may have seen, the latter's "Human Time" is specifically said to be lacking a forelock ("with foretop bald and high"), which reflects the passive, moonlike state of receptivity he represents—an apt image of Coleridge's own spiritual state at the time, no doubt, but one whose unflinching self-honesty ("As 'twere," "He seems," "which seems"), including sexual candor ("they shrink in as Moles / Nature's mute monks"—line 6) and pathos, as well as some vision, attains once more to the level of the androgynous sublime.[24]

Blake remarks that "the productions of our youth and our maturer age are equal" in all essentials;[25] and it seems appropriate to conclude this discussion of Coleridge's androgynous sublimity with some further reference to his most characteristic poem, which I have more fully discussed elsewhere, and which, like some of the early portraits, presents him in his most memorable role.

The persona or poet-hero of "Kubla Khan," who proposes to recreate the Golden Age as symbolized by an artful evocation of thirteenth-century Xanadu in the reader's mind, is a beautiful, androgynous but virile youth whose "flashing eyes [and] floating hair" (50) contain more than a touch of self-portraiture, whether deliberately done or otherwise. Dorothy Wordsworth has testified to her first impression of Coleridge's "poet's eye in a fine frenzy rolling," sensual mouth, and glossy, black, pendulous hair in her well-known account of their meeting not long before "Kubla Khan" was written.[26] Coleridge, whose poetic persona also emphasizes the importance of his *soror mystica* or Muse, the Abyssinian Maid, is anticipating an insight that the second generation of romantics further developed, and one that I wish to explore more fully in the latter part of this study, namely that the poet *qua* poet is either androgynous, or not truly sublime.

In "Kubla Khan" the pleasure-dome, together with its shadow or reflection, which "[f]loated midway on the waves" (32) of the sacred river, make up a circular or ovoid shape that not only reminds one of Plato's androgynous egg, but is also, as Coleridge knew, a Sanskrit symbol of God.[27] Further, the poem's symbolic structure may include a buried Christian reference insofar as the name of the fountain-fed Alph, thrice referred to as "the sacred river," and the shape of its counterpart the dome, together with the latter's reflection in the water, suggest the phrase "Alpha and Omega" with which Jesus several times identifies himself in the vision of Saint John the Divine: "I am Alpha and Omega, the beginning and the end. I will give unto him that is athirst of the fountain of the water of life freely."[28]

Like the serpentine course of the sacred river Alph "[f]ive miles meandering with a mazy motion" (25), such water imagery implicitly combines masculine and feminine qualities. "Weave a circle round him thrice" (51) means in effect to weave around the inspired poet-prophet an androgynous ovoid aura, a concept to be more fully discussed in the conclusion. Similarly, the "honey-dew" and "milk of Paradise" that the protagonist is said to have eaten and drunk in the last two lines are at once sacramental and androgynous, the former recalling the manna (cf. the phrase "honey wild, and manna dew" in Keats's "La Belle Dame Sans Merci") with which Jehovah fed the wandering Israelites, and the latter sounding unmistakably feminine, although also perhaps latently homoerotic, in its connotations. Thus the analogical has been subsumed by the androgynous sublime.

4

Byron's Sublime Androgyny

Byron's Feminine Nature

FROM AN AD HOMINEM PERSPECTIVE—THE ONLY KIND MOST PEOPLE are interested in anymore—Byron's bisexuality makes him the major English poet most germane to the motif of the androgyne, if not the mode of the sublime. For instance, we know that some of Byron's early love poems, such as the ones "To Thyrza," once thought to have been addressed to a girl, were actually written about a choirboy, John Edleston, who died young.[1] It seems fair to assume that Byron's experience as a bisexual gave him a certain ambience when it came to dealing with the theme of the fundamental unity of the sexes.

The word *bisexual,* like *androgyne,* is semantically ambiguous: it can mean "having the organs of both sexes," or "attracted by both sexes" *(OED).* In Blake's myth we have noticed the polar opposition of the hermaphrodite and androgyne figures, the former having satanic, the latter redemptive connotations. We have also observed Blake's delicate, sympathetic allusions to homosexuality—e.g., in his reference to "Shiloh the Emanation of France" (*J,* 55:27). Byron is, interestingly enough, the only contemporary poet to whom Blake alludes by name in his published works: *The Ghost of Abel* (1822) is significantly addressed "To LORD BYRON in the Wilderness." This late work, a two-page pamphlet complete with engraved illustrations, is Blake's reply to Byron's *Cain,* which had appeared in December 1821 and shocked the orthodox religious establishment with its portrayal of a tyrannical Creator rejoicing in cruelty, the author of sin, death, and hell.

Blake addresses Byron as Elijah ("What doest thou here, Elijah?"), harking back to his portrayals of Rintrah and Edom (Esau) in *The Marriage of Heaven and Hell.* These are all types of prophetic wrath, and Blake is hailing Byron as a true poet whose vision is not so much wrong as incomplete. For Blake, unlike Byron, interpreted the mark that Jehovah placed on Cain's forehead as the kiss of forgiveness, as we know from his illuminated copy of *Genesis*. Abel's Ghost is a form of Satan the Accuser vainly crying for vengeance, as Blake in effect rewrites the last scene of Byron's play and reclaims his "mystery" as an aspect of the everlasting gospel, which includes not only forgiveness—which Cain had successfully evoked from his dying brother—but also self-forgiveness, which Cain explicitly rejects: hence his continuing torment.

This ethical and metaphysical excursus may serve as a useful prolegomenon to an investigation of the androgynous sublime in Byron if we for a moment focus on the role of Adah, Cain's sister and wife, or what Blake would have called his emanation. (The situation recalls Byron's relations with half-sister, Augusta, and the name "Adah" resembles that of Byron's daughter Ada.) In an important stage direction twenty or so lines from the end of the play, "ADAH stoops down and kisses the body of ABEL."[2] Since Coleridge had observed in his prose poem "The Wanderings of Cain" the psychological paradox that the victim partakes of the guilt of the murderer, Adah's action is equivalent to the kiss of forgiveness. She then offers to share Cain's burden of guilt with him, and as they prepare to go "Eastward from Eden" with their children, she says to Cain, "thou shalt by be my guide, and may *our* God / Be *thine*" (emphasis added). There is deliberate semantic ambiguity as well as subtle irony to this, as Adah is really assuming the role of Cain's spiritual preceptor. She is trying to heal with love the division in Cain between an imaginative God and the Accuser within, and she thus represents the only real hope for Cain's future development as the play ends.

The concept of woman as man's spiritual preceptor, particularly in times of crisis, runs throughout Byron's poetry, combined (as I have shown elsewhere[3]) with the myth of the Golden Age. One thinks of Byron's poems to Augusta written shortly after his separation from Lady Byron, with the former assuming the role of a tutelary spirit inducting the socially alienated poet into the ways of nature:

> In the desert a fountain is springing,
>   In the wide waste there still is a tree,
> And a bird in the solitude singing,
>   Which speaks to my spirit of *thee*.
>
>   ("Stanzas to Augusta," 45–49)

Byron and the Byronic hero both discovered nature as a sort of super-female emanation at Lake Leman (the Lake of Geneva), where Byron met Shelley, who gave him purgative doses of Wordsworth, and where both poets spent the summer of 1816 (which is ironically still referred to by locals as "the year without a summer" because of the bad weather). Byron's poetry of this period is likewise overcast. The ecological awareness of his poignant poem "The Prisoner of Chillon" may be seen in the quasi-androgynous context already intimated, as may Byron's interesting personification of the title figure in the concluding half-line of the apocalyptic poem "Darkness"—"She was the Universe"—with its hint of a new mythology, if not of a new cosmic order. One is reminded of a saying of Alan Watts: "If the light implies the darkness, the darkness also implies the light."[4] The negative sublime of "Darkness" adumbrates the more positive sublime of the famous apostrophe to Ocean with which Byron's peripatetic tour de force *Childe Harold's Pilgrimage* comes to its impressive climax. It may be useful to approach this Pisgah-height of Byron's verse via the memorable description of the storm over Lake Leman in canto 3, which, insofar as it is beheld at night, provides a valid link with the theme of "Darkness":

> The sky is changed!—and such a change!* Oh night,
> And storm, and darkness, ye are wondrous strong,
> Yet lovely in your strength, as is the light
> Of a dark eye in woman.
>
> (860–63)

Darkness, once more personified as feminine, this time is also said to be "lovely," confirming to a degree one's supposition of a latent positive underside to the seemingly nihilistic ending of the earlier poem. Further, in his footnote to this stanza Byron juxtaposes the words "terrible" and "beautiful" in a way that at once evokes Burke and subverts him. Byron is implicitly objecting to Burke's bifurcation of the sublime and the beautiful, and attempting to restore the androgynous unity of the aesthetic experience.[5]

Byron exults in describing the storm, complete with lightning and "live thunder," as it were embracing the eternal feminine principle it represents, including love and sexuality, and portraying this

---

*"The thunder-storm to which these lines refer occurred on the 13th of June, 1816, at midnight. I have seen . . . several more terrible, but none more beautiful" (Byron's note).

principle as an objective correlative of the destructive underside of genius, with which he and Shelley were equally fascinated:

> And this is in the night!—Most glorious night!
> Thou wert not sent for slumber! let me be
> A sharer in thy fierce and far delight,—
> A portion of the tempest and of thee!
> How the lit lake shines, a phosphoric sea,
> And the big rain comes dancing to the earth!
> And now again 'tis black,—and now, the glee
> Of the loud hills shakes with its mountain-mirth,
> As if they did rejoice o'er a young earthquake's birth.
>
> (869–77)

"Mountain-mirth," rhyming as it does with "birth," echoes and parodies the last stanza of Coleridge's "Dejection: an Ode," and the following stanza employs another Coleridgean trope with a difference, that of the heights on either side of the Rhone as "lovers who have parted," echoing "Christabel" (421–22), for whose long-delayed publication Byron had recently played the part of poetic godfather. Byron is of course alluding to his own separation from Lady Byron and once more exploring the paradox that love—like genius—has a destructive underside: "Love was the very root of the fond rage / Which blighted their life's bloom" (883–84). Only the androgynous poet and the lover (both "of imagination all compact," as Shakespeare's Theseus had put it) can grasp the blade of this mystery, which, like the "swift Rhone cleaves [its] way" (887) between the sundered halves, the river of life—and death—itself.

The apostrophe to Ocean with which canto 4 of *Childe Harold* concludes is prefaced by two important stanzas, in the first of which (177) Byron alludes to Augusta as the "one fair Spirit" for whom he would consider the world well lost. This is followed by the stanza containing the notorious line "I love not Man the less, but Nature more," in which Augusta, by implication at least, becomes once more an epitome of nature in a manner somewhat reminiscent of the Wordsworth set.

Because Byron's relations with Augusta were quasi-incestuous and, in part at least, responsible for the breakup of his marriage, the motif of the destructiveness of love and genius is brought to a focus in these two stanzas preceding the famous apostrophe to Ocean. The sea has long been recognized as both a feminine principle connected with love and procreation (one thinks of the birth of Venus) as well as, in more recent psychological theory, a symbol of the unconscious mind or chaos, the destructive element in which genius sometimes delights to immerse itself, as Blake had observed in *The Marriage of Heaven and Hell.*

Unlike Wordsworth, who tended to hear in the ocean's roar the patriarchal voice of the returned judgmental Christ, Byron portrays Ocean as implicitly androgynous, as well as refreshingly playful: "Spurning him [man] from thy bosom to the skies, / And send'st him, shivering in thy playful spray" (1616–17). (Compare the reference two stanzas further on to "thy wild waves' play.") I say "implicitly androgynous" because the wonderful line "Time writes no wrinkle on thine azure brow" (1637) contains more than a hint of narcissistic self-portraiture, Byron's smooth, marble brow having become legendary even during his lifetime.

Thus, Byron portrays Ocean as a symbol of eternity—"Such as creation's dawn beheld, thou rollest now" (1639)—and also of the feminine aspect of God: "Thou glorious mirror, where the Almighty's form / Glasses itself in tempests" (1639–40). One is reminded of the Wisdom (in Greek, Sophia) mentioned in the Book of Proverbs: "The Lord possessed me in the beginning of his way, before his works of old" (8:22). This passage has been much discussed in mystical writings, such as those of Jacob Boehme.

According to Boehme, after God arose from the *Ungrund* or Abyss, the creation of heaven or the unfallen world began when the will of God contemplated itself in the looking-glass of God's wisdom, which Boehme calls the Virgin Sophia because it engenders nothing but reflects the images of all things.

> The Eternal Virgin of Wisdom stood in Paradise as a Figure, in which all the *Wonders* of God were known . . . and in the Virgin God created the matrix of the Earth, so that it was a *palapable Image* in substance, and all, whatsoever liveth and moveth was in one Image . . . for that virgin is eternally uncreated and ungenerated: It is the Wisdom of God and Image of the Deity.[6]

Byron, who would have come across references to Boehme in the notes to Coleridge's recently published *Biographia Literaria,* if not elsewhere, echoes the conceit, describing Ocean as God's "glorious mirror," but he also (in contrast to Boehme) characteristically endows the figure with darkness, sexuality and fecundity:

> Dark-heaving;—boundless, endless and sublime—
> The image of Eternity—the throne
> Of the Invisible; even from out thy slime

The monsters of the deep are made; each zone
Obeys thee; thou goest forth, dread, fathomless, alone.

(1643–47)

Here Ocean becomes once more androgynous, with "Dark-heaving" bosom (compare the ending of "Darkness") and genital slime, engendering "monsters" as well as, by implication at least, men and women in her image, which is itself the image of the Creator:

> The Lord possessed me in the beginning of his way, before the works of old.
> I was set up from everlasting, from the beginning, or ever the earth was.
> When there were no depths, I was brought forth; when there were no fountains abounding with water.
> (Prov. 8:22–24)

The passage from Proverbs is unquestionably more "chaste" than Byron's apostrophe, but it is arguable that the latter is equally sublime: Byron deliberately uses the word *sublime* (1643), which he had formerly eschewed. The verse owes much of its rhetorical effectiveness to the use of long "o" sounds—a trick Byron may have picked up from Milton's sonnet "On the Late Massacre in Piedmont," whose patriarchal invocation of vengeance he cunningly inverts (Byron loves Ocean, for all her destructiveness) along with certain dualistic eighteenth-century concepts of sublimity.

In addition to the theme of the poet's imaginative identification with the spirit of the seemingly destructive ocean, anticipating Shelley's "Ode to the West Wind," there is the pettiness and vanity of much of the panorama of human history when measured against this image of eternity. This contrast is the essence of the Byronic androgynous sublime, in which nature becomes a symbol of a higher mode of existence participating in the power and glory of divine creativity and freedom.

The theme of the divine analogue—the idea that human creativity participates in divine creativity, which Byron may have picked up from Coleridge—is also evident when Byron brings his sublime discourse down to earth by means of a frankly autobiographical touch:

> And I have loved thee, Ocean! and my joy
> Of youthful sports was on thy breast to be

> Borne, like thy bubbles, onward: from a boy
> I wantoned with thy breakers—they to me
> Were a delight; and if the freshening sea
> Made them a terror—'twas a pleasing fear,
> For I was as it were a child of thee,
> And trusted to thy billows far and near,
> And laid my hand upon thy mane—as I do here.
>
> (1648–56)

The last of these lines echoes Genesis (1:2)—"And the Spirit of God moved upon the face of the waters"—thus identifying human with divine creativity, as well as conflating this idea with the passage we have been discussing from Proverbs. Once more, Byron is insisting upon the element of playfulness in creation and Creation. Compare the voice of old:

> When he gave to the sea his decree, that the waters should not pass his commandment: when he appointed the foundation of the earth:
> Then I was by him, as one brought up with him: and was daily his delight, rejoicing always before him:
> Rejoicing in the habitable part of the earth; and my delights were with the sons of men.
>
> (Prov. 8:29–31)

Byron's "pleasing fear" (1653)—which may have been for him the beginning of wisdom—is the oxymoronic equivalent of the androgynous sublime, itself a subtle combination of purging and play in which the alert reader is invited to participate. When Byron says he was a child of Ocean "borne" (1650) on her breast, there is again a hint of androgyny as he punningly invokes the birth of Venus. Compare the sexually charged oxymoron "freshening sea," combining brackishness with fecundity.

There is also word-play beneath the seeming solemnity of the poem's conclusion: "Farewell! with *him* [Harold] alone may rest the pain, / If such there were—with *you*, the moral of his strain!" (1673–74) The mention of "pain" and the final low-keyed pun on "strain" suggest an androgynous parallel between writing poetry and giving physical birth: Byron's verse in *Childe Harold* has more subtlety of texture, and hence greater ambience, than it is sometimes given credit for having.

Manfred as Destroyer and Preserver

Manfred, which Byron conceived and began writing amid the Bernese Alps, where the scenery and the people are about equally

wild, is a Gothic "dramatic poem" on the theme of the doppel-
gänger, in this instance represented by Manfred's (probable) sister
Astarte, for whose recent death he feels somehow responsible. (In
Thun Castle, which Byron would have seen during his journey
through the Bernese Oberland, a local count had murdered his
brother during the fourteenth century.[7]) On the biographical level
there can be little doubt that Byron is exorcizing the ghost of his
love affair with Augusta, which had socially "destroyed" her, and
also killing off an aspect of his relations with Lady Byron in the
complex handling of the curse towards the end of the opening
scene.

A good deal of the charm of the Alps—as of Ocean—for Byron
consisted in what may be termed their amoral sublimity, or com-
mingling of apparently innocent beauty with destructiveness.
Scene 2 finds Manfred atop the Jungfrau ("Maiden"), remarking
on the beauty of the scene so reminiscent of the Golden Age (the
"patriarchal days" of line 49). Byron had climbed the adjacent
Lauberhorn (his "Wengren Mountain") and made similar remarks
in his journal: "the whole of the day [23 September 1816] as fine
in point of weather as the day on which Paradise was made."[8]
When Manfred contrasts his lot with that of the supposedly innocent Chamois-hunter—who, like the eagle of line 31, is also a
predatory creature—one cannot help but note that he is exaggerating his own guilt in the typical Gothic fashion.

Similarly, Astarte is said to have resembled Manfred "in linea-
ments" (2.2.105), which suggests that she also resembled him in
other ways; in other words, she may not have been an unwilling
respondent in the circumstances involving real or implied incest
that led to her death. Astarte (or Ashtoreth, originally the Babylo-
nian Ishtar) was the Semitic Venus, a fertility goddess mentioned
in the Old Testament. She was identified with the moon (compare
Manfred's farewell address to the Moon [3.4.1–44]) and her worship was sometimes orgiastic. It is regarded in the Bible as a type
of wickedness. But Byron, while never denying a sexual aspect,
always maintained that his relationship with Augusta was essentially based on pure love: hence, to a degree, he "spiritualizes" his
portrayal of Astarte in *Manfred*. This is in accord with the romantic conception of sexual love as a coming together of consenting
spirits, itself an important aspect of the androgynous sublime.

In the most enchanting scene from *Manfred* (2.2) Byron portrays
the Witch of the Alps, a beautiful androgynous figure who is really
a counterpart of Byron himself. She appears to Manfred beneath
the arch of the sunbow caused by the refraction of the sun's rays

in the spray thrown up by the torrent of Steinbach Falls, which would have been much more impressive during the extremely wet summer of 1816, before the glaciers began to recede, than it is now. Manfred begins by addressing the Witch as a "Beautiful Spirit" with "hair of light," "dazzling eyes of glory," and "celestial aspect" (13–23). As Byron's account of the Witch develops, one can perceive more than a touch of self-portraiture:

> Beautiful Spirit! in thy calm clear brow,
> Wherein in glass'd serenity of soul,
> Which of itself shows immortality,
> I read that thou wilt pardon to a Son
> Of Earth.
>
> (2.2.25–29)

By portraying the Witch androgynously, complete with noble Byronic brow, Byron is able to have Manfred invoke her "pardon" and aid in summoning up the spirit of Astarte without swearing allegiance to her: she is not a goddess but a subordinate spirit, who nevertheless presents a parallel with the antediluvian "giant sons" with whom Manfred identifies later, in his farewell address to the Sun:

> Glorious orb! the idol
> Of early nature, and the vigorous race
> Of undiseased mankind, the giant sons
> Of the embrace of angels, with a sex
> More beautiful than they, which did draw down
> The erring spirits who can ne'er return.
>
> (3.2.3–8)

Byron is said to have remarked to Lady Byron during their honeymoon that he felt a special affinity for these giant sons of God, who are mentioned in Genesis (6:1–4) and also in the apocryphal Book of Enoch.[9] Hence Manfred's "refusal to bow," and his equation of feminine beauty with masculine—more properly, androgynous—sublimity.

The drama ends with Manfred refusing the good offices of the Abbot of Saint Maurice in his patriarchal or ecclesiastical role, but instead offering *him* a sort of maternal-cum-fraternal aid and comfort on the human level paralleling his concern for Astarte:

Man.   . . . Away!

Abbot.   Thou dost not mean to menace me?

Man.   Not I;
          I simply tell thee peril is at hand,
          And *would preserve thee . . .*
                              Fare thee well—
          Give me thy hand. . . .
          Old Man! 'tis not so difficult to die.

                              (3.4.55–151; emphasis added)

Manfred, the erstwhile destroyer, has become the androgynous preserver.

Androgynous Sublimity in *Don Juan*

The concept of the androgynous preserver is also an important leitmotif in *Don Juan,* where the conventionalized ladykilling Byronic hero is finally stood on his head. (In *Beppo,* Byron's brilliant trial run for *Don Juan,* the eponymous quasi-Byronic hero becomes "androgynized"—and humanized—by being cuckolded.) Byron's psychological insight that women typically take the lead in sexual relations—itself prefigured in Shakespeare's *Othello,* "Upon this hint I spake" (1.3.166)—enables him to construct a new kind of poem in which women, as coprotectors of life and culture, by and large have an equal say with men.

This becomes evident in Byron's portrayal of Donna Julia, with whom young Juan has his first love affair: "A little still she strove, and much repented, / And whispering 'I will ne'er consent'—consented" (1.935–36). At this point in the narrative, midway through the first canto, the poem "breaks open" and begins to become truly androgynous, in the sense that it attains a double perspective on sexual and social relations. Julia, involved in the wrong kind of marriage, is not so much being satirized for what may seem her logical inconsistency, as admired for her daring in saying "Yes!" to life in all its manifold complexity. One is reminded by anticipation of Molly Bloom's soliloquy in the last chapter of Joyce's *Ulysses.* Byron's satire, as the previous stanza (116) indicates, is really directed at Plato and like-minded rationalists—among whom must be included Juan's mother, Donna Inez—for trying to drive a wedge between human thought and feeling.

Accordingly, when Julia's jealous, suspicious husband and his minions discover her sitting up in bed, with young Juan hidden between her legs (an interestingly androgynous as well as "birthing" image) she rises magnificently to the occasion by delivering an improvised smokescreen of a harangue that extends for some twelve stanzas without a break. Here is Byron's portrayal of woman as the protectress and nurturer of human values—including life and love—adumbrating the portrayals of Haidée in canto 2 and Neuha in *The Island*. Julia's very name renders her a sort of double of Juan: her necessarily voluble duplicity also coincides with her role as androgynous "destroyer"—rebel against social conventions—and preserver of what is really valid beneath those conventions.

The same is true of Julia's farewell letter, written to Juan from the convent where her jealous husband has immured her, in which she protests against the double-standard of a male-dominated society but remains true to the principle of love, symbolized by the sunflower seal on her letter, a central image of the poem. Unlike the "Youth pined away with desire, / And the pale Virgin shrouded in snow" of Blake's poem "Ah! Sun flower," Julia and Juan *have* dared to seek the fulfilment offered by an illicit love. The significance of Julia's sunflower motto—"Elle vous suit partout" (1.1582)—is that, although victimized by a hypocritical and unjust society, she too has attained a sort of fulfilment through having initiated Juan into the ways of love, and hence will share vicariously in his subsequent adventures. Thus Byron contrives to invert the Don Juan legend, or rather turn it inside out. Love, like virtue, is seen to be its own reward.

Canto 2, as I and others have shown, is structured upon the myth of the Golden Age, and its most compelling character is of course Haidée, the best of Byron's heroines. The motif of the androgyne is introduced when Byron hints at a reversal of conventional roles in his portrayal of Haidée's reaction upon catching her first sight of Juan:

> And walking out upon the beach, below
>   The cliff, towards sunset, on that day she found,
> Insensible,—not dead, but nearly so,—
>   Don Juan, almost famish'd, and half drown'd;
> But being naked, she was shock'd, you know,
>   Yet deem'd herself in common pity bound,
> As far as in her lay, 'to take him in,
> A stranger' dying, with so white a skin.
>
>   (2.1025–32)

Juan has been washed up on the island naked, like Ulysses, but Haidée is less shocked ("you know") than fascinated by his helplessness and pale nudity. The subtle eroticism of this is in accord with Byron's perception of women taking the lead in establishing sexual relations.

The cave in which Haidée and her maid Zoe nurse Juan back to health—anticipating Neuha's cave in *The Island,* which serves a similar function—is also, in its ovoid shape, reminiscent of Plato's myth of the androgyne. They cover Juan temporarily with their petticoats (2.1061), a bit of cross-dressing that further develops the androgynous motif. This motif extends to dietary matters: in the same stanza (133), Haidée and Zoe provide the famished Juan with a breakfast of "eggs, coffee, bread, and fish," a diet that is later expanded to include fruit, honey, and "Scio wine" (2.1160). Still later in the canto Byron expands upon the theory behind this meatless regimen:

> Any every morn his colour freshlier came,
>   And every day help'd on his convalescence;
> 'Twas well, because health in the human frame
>   Is pleasant, besides being true love's essence,
> For health and idleness to passion's flame
>   Are oil and gunpowder; and some good lessons
> And also learnt from Ceres and from Bacchus,
> Without whom Venus will not long attack us.
>
> While Venus fills the heart (without heart really
>   Love, though good always, is not quite so good)
> Ceres presents a plate of vermicelli,—
>   For love must be sustain'd like flesh and blood,—
> While Bacchus pours out wine, or hands a jelly:
>   Eggs, oysters too, are amatory food;
> But who is their purveyor from above
> Heaven knows,—it may be Neptune, Pan, or Jove.
>   (2.1345–60)

In the first of these stanzas the goddess of food and the god of wine are seen as acolytes of the goddess of love. Juan's diet, like Byron's own, tends toward vegetarianism partly because the latter believed that a meat diet, such as that favored by the English, makes people warlike (2.1225–48). One is also reminded by contrast of the cannibalism of the sailors mentioned earlier in this canto (617–32) who die a horrible death, and of Juan's praiseworthy abstinence. Unlike most of Byron's earlier heroes, Juan is—to use the current idiom—notably nonmacho.[10]

Not surprisingly, Byron also invokes the myth of the androgyne in his portrayal of the love-play of Juan and Haidée:

> They look upon each other, and their eyes
>   Gleam in the moonlight; and her white arms clasps
> Round Juan's head, and his around her lies
>   Half buried in the tresses which it grasps;
> She sits upon his knee, and drinks his sighs,
>   He hers, until they end in broken gasps;
> And thus they form a group that's quite antique,
> Half naked, loving, natural, and Greek.
>
>   (2.1545–52)

The use of the words *round* and *around* as well as the double use of *half*—once at the beginning of the fourth line, and once at the beginning of line eight—have structural and symbolic connotations that remind one of Plato's poetic parable of the egg-shaped androgyne in the *Symposium*. The stanza as a whole deals with an aspect of Plato's idea that "human nature was originally one and we were a whole, and the desire and pursuit of the whole is called love."[11] It should go without saying that this is the most sublime canto of *Don Juan:* "And they were happy, for to their young eyes / Each was an angel, and earth paradise" (2.1631–32).

The most famous single passage in *Don Juan,* and the most sublime in the conventional or "phallic" sense, is the set piece beginning "The Isles of Greece, the Isles of Greece!" in canto 3, which consists of sixteen six-line stanzas differing markedly from the rest of the poem (689–784). These stanzas are doubly phallic insofar as they are a kind of patriotic war song, or song of national liberation, such as Byron had heard sung by Andreas Londos at Vostitza in the Peloponnesus in 1809.[12] Byron deliberately undercuts them, and hence the sort of sublime they epitomize, by having them sung at Haidée and Juan's feast by a turncoat poet, who is loosely modeled on Byron's favorite satiric target, laureate Southey. By devaluing, at least to a degree, the phallic sublime of this set piece, Byron is not only signaling to the reader his personal reservations about war, alluded to earlier in the poem—even, it would seem, war in a "just cause"—but also (more germane to the present study) his reaction against the phallic sublime of parts of *Childe Harold,* such as the descriptions of the Battle of Waterloo, in favor of what we have been calling the androgynous sublime.

Byron manages to have it both ways by intimating that the turncoat poet is himself an ambivalent figure who is attempting to regain something of the sincerity of his youth by agreeing "to a short armistice with Truth" (664). As Byron's narrator also remarks after the turncoat poet's song has been sung, "his strain display'd some feeling—right or wrong" (789); but the rest of this stanza further develops Byron's ambivalence toward the phallic sublime and thus subtly reinforces the poem's focus on the Juan-Haidée relationship and the androgynous sublime as its symbolic and rhetorical center.

The motif of cross-dressing (of which the term "turncoat" may be seen as a sort of verbal surrogate) in *Don Juan* has been discussed by Susan J. Wolfson in an interesting article,[13] but is only tangentially related to the theme of the androgynous sublime. The former motif, as Wolfson has shown, runs throughout the poem, but the latter virtually ceases as a rhetorical device after the death of Haidée, although its lingering effect is constantly felt as a sort of measuring rod. Wolfson approvingly quotes Derrida's remark that to cross the "line of demarcation," whether in terms of gender or genre, is to "risk impurity, anomaly, or monstrosity."[14] She also quotes with approval the well-known passage from Deuteronomy (22:5) about all forms of cross-dressing being "an abomination unto the LORD" (one would give much to have Shakespeare's views on that passage), and adds her own neomoralist updating: "A feminized Juan always invites death into the poem, whether in the form of threats to his own life or the lives of those implicated in his travesties."[15] Wolfson neglects to mention that there is abundant evidence of death in the poem unrelated to Juan's "feminization": one thinks of the shipwreck early in canto 2 and the seige of Ismail in cantos 7 and 8. Byron seems to have foreseen the critical tendency to oversolemnize *Don Juan,* and warns his readers against it, for instance, by prefacing cantos 6 to 8 (originally published together as a single installment of the poem) with the famous "cakes and ale" passage from *Twelfth Night.*

Most of the poem's cross-dressing takes place in the harem scenes of cantos 5 and 6, which are basically meant to be good fun. The only such incident that seems to have any profound significance—an impression deriving partly from its position near the end of the poem—is the Duchess of Fitz-Fulke's disguising herself as the Black Friar (in canto 16) in order to consummate her seduction of Juan. Fitz-Fulke takes Juan, who is in the process of falling in love with Aurora Raby (a sort of reincarnation of Haidée, insofar as she too has Edenic associations) by surprise, while he is thinking of Aurora, and effectively seduces him. Fitz-Fulke is portrayed not as the sexual initiator but as the sexual predator, and in this instance her strategic sensuality disguises itself as not merely masculinity, but also spirituality:

> But still the Shade remained; the blue eyes glared,
>   And rather variably for stony death;

> Yet one thing rather good the grave had spared,
>> The Ghost had a remarkably sweet breath.
> A straggling curl showed he had been fairhaired;
>> A red lip, with two rows of pearls beneath,
> Gleamed forth, as through the casement's ivy shroud
> The Moon peeped, just escaped from a grey cloud. . . .
>
> The ghost, if ghost it were, seemed a sweet soul
>> As ever lurked beneath a holy hood;
> A dimpled chin, a neck of ivory, stole
>> Forth into something much like flesh and blood;
> Back fell the sable frock and dreary cowl,
>> And they revealed—alas! that e'er they should!
> In full, voluptuous, but *not o'er*grown bulk,
> The phantom of her frolic Grace-Fitz-Fulke!

$$(16.1009-32)$$

One is reminded by this description of Coleridge's "Night-mare LIFE-IN-DEATH . . . / Who thicks man's blood with cold," from *The Ancient Mariner* (193–94). Points that both passages have in common are blond hair, whiteness of skin, red lips, loose morals, and the apparition of feminine beauty instilling fear, as of something spectral.

Byron's clever parody evokes a kind of *frisson* not unlike that of its Coleridgean counterpart, except that here there is an undercurrent of Byronic mocking laughter, directed not primarily at Coleridge (whose masterpiece Byron in fact admired), but at what he saw as an aspect of the rotting Regency society, England's ancien régime. The result is the negative sublime, negative insofar as the subject matter is dislocated androgyny. Juan, who comes downstairs for breakfast next morning "with his virgin face" (17.104), shares in this dislocation, looking as though he has combated "with more than one" ghost—shades of Haidée?—as the fragment breaks off.

One may conclude that Byron's exploration of the mode and motif of the androgynous sublime, interrupted as it was by his untimely death, ends with a moral wrapped inside an enigma, but that when due allowance is made for his use of satire and ironic displacement, he remained remarkably true to the theme that constitutes the subject of this book.[16]

5

Shelley's Androgynous Quest

Voice and Vision

THOMAS JEFFERSON HOGG, ONE OF SHELLEY'S EARLIEST DISCI-
ples, recalls that upon first meeting Shelley he nearly broke off
relations with him because he found the poet's voice "intolerably
shrill, harsh and discordant; of the most cruel intension. It was
perpetual and without any remission; it excoriated my ears."[1] This
impression, particularly Hogg's reference to shrillness and harsh-
ness combined with volubility, which has been corroborated by
others, suggests that Shelley's voice and manner of speaking combined (as Coleridge, in another context, said the poetic imagination
should do) opposite or discordant qualities. This presents a significant analogy with an important aspect of the present study, namely
the concept of the poet as androgyne.

Francis Thompson, in what is still the best brief essay on Shelley,
draws attention to his childlike quality: "both as a poet and man
he was essentially a child."[2] We have observed that the child *qua*
child is androgynous, like the poet *qua* poet. Shelley, whose first
love affair was with Hogg (according to his most recent biographer)
and who later became Byron's poetic friend and rival, was interested, at least theoretically, in the theme of bisexuality.[3] For instance his "Sonnet to Byron," left unpublished at the time of his
death, concludes with a perhaps half-conscious homoerotic double
entendre: "the worm beneath the sod / May lift itself in homage to
the God."[4] "Sod" is English schoolboy slang for sodomite, and
Shelley in this late poem is at least facing up to what he might
have earlier repressed or denied. The same holds true, *mutatis
mutandis,* for Shelley's androgynous impulses.

Shelley's first accomplished poem, "Alastor, or the Spirit of Solitude" (1815), deals, as its title suggests, with the theme of poetic
isolation, which includes sexual isolation. The significantly un-
named Poet-protagonist, during his wanderings throughout the Ori-

ent (as the Middle East was known at this time), becomes engaged in the ironic pursuit of a nympholeptic vision that he already possesses, rejects the sexual advances of a lovelorn Arab maiden, and suffers accordingly, meeting an untimely death.

Shelley's preface to the poem, in which he ironically quotes Wordsworth against Wordsworth ("The good die first, / And those whose hearts are dry as summer dust, / Burn to the socket!"), is an attempt to distance himself from both the influence of Wordsworth and his alienated persona, with whom he identifies emotionally but not intellectually. The poem may also show the influence of Blake's *Book of Thel,* which Shelley could have seen through his contact with the Godwin household, and is likewise organized around the myth of Narcissus, who represented the wrong (because incomplete) kind of androgyny. Thus the forty-nine-line conclusion "mirrors" the forty-nine-line introduction, and leaves one with the sense of a genius with a missing gene.

In spite of their "progressive" themes, such as vegetarianism, women's liberation, and the renovation of society—ideas that Shelley had imbibed from William Godwin's *Political Justice* and Mary Wollstonecraft's *Rights of Woman*—his poems do not become truly androgynous until his middle period following his elopement with Mary Wollstonecraft Godwin and the crucial meeting with Byron at Lake Leman in the summer of 1816. The watershed poem is less "Mont Blanc"—an "effusion," as Shelley rightly called it, with an uneasy mélange of Godwinism and Platonism—than "Hymn to Intellectual Beauty," wherein Shelley makes a clean break with Godwinian materialism in favour of Neoplatonic idealism and the worship of supreme beauty (which Keats also identified with Truth), the inspirer of all beautiful thought and action.

There is a couplet in this poem that has grated on some readers' sensibilities, as it once grated on mine: "Sudden thy shadow fell on me; / I shrieked, and clasped my hands in ecstasy" (59–60). Now whatever one may think of the tone of this—it is clearly meant to be ecstatic—one cannot deny that Shelley is here "speaking" in his own voice, as so memorably described by Hogg: "intolerably shrill, harsh and discordant." The following lines, in which Shelley recalls his youthful vow of self-dedication to becoming a poet of liberation, complete with "beating heart and streaming eyes" (63), continue with newfound confidence and self-honesty to evoke a synthesis of masculine and feminine qualities in the pursuit of this quest. From this point on in Shelley's career, the poet as androgyne replaces the poet as theoretician.

Something of the same newfound confidence can be seen in the

handling of the brother-sister incest theme, itself a kind of androgynous metaphor, in Shelley's longest poem, *Laon and Cythna,*
which he wrote during a sojourn in England in 1817, and which
was finally published a year later (with the incest motif "toned
down," to get it past the censors) under the intriguing title *The
Revolt of Islam.* Cythna, who has been called "the first 'new
woman' in English poetry"[5]—a designation more properly belong-
ing to Blake's Oothoon—is at one point abducted for a Turkish
seraglio and leads a revolution in Constantinople. In the revised
version Cythna says she will be a "friend and sister" (3360) to
Laon, her lover, thus preserving something of the incest motif.
Shelley, doubtless recalling some of his conversations with Byron,
proclaimed incest a very poetical subject because it represents the
mind communing with itself in the act of creation.[6] So too, with
less trouble one might add, androgyny.

The madman who appears in the latter part of "Julian and Maddalo," Shelley's urbane, avant-garde poem about one of his lengthy
conversations with Byron, is an androgyne in everything but name.
The madman, whom Julian-Shelley and Maddalo-Byron visit in his
cell, has forgiven the lady who rejected him, and he has cast away
"all revenge, all pride" (502), thus fulfilling the psychological condi-
tions for a restoration of the Golden Age, if only others would do
likewise. Byron-Maddalo sees the madman as a sort of poet
manqué:

> [Maddalo] said: 'Most wretched men
> Are cradled into poetry by wrong,
> They learn in suffering what they teach in song.'
>
> (544–56)

Julian-Shelley remarks upon the "deep tenderness" that the maniac
has wrought within him.

In the sequel the madman's lady, her pride likewise humbled,
briefly returns to visit him, as recounted to Julian years later by
Maddalo's then-six-year-old daughter, who witnessed the event,
and whom Shelley compares to "one of Shakespeare's women"
(594), those earlier essays in androgyny. Thus Maddalo's daughter
(in real life Allegra, who died in a convent at the age of five, Byron's natural daughter by Claire Clairmont) and the madman are
counterparts, both innocent victims whose endurance and compassion remind one by anticipation of the sublime ending of *Prometheus Unbound:*

> To suffer woes which Hope thinks infinite;
> To forgive wrongs darker than death or night;
> To defy Power, which seems omnipotent;
> To love, and bear; to hope till Hope creates
> From its own wreck the thing it contemplates;
> Neither to change, nor falter, nor repent;
> This, like thy glory, Titan, is to be
> Good, great and joyous, beautiful and free;
> This is alone Life, Joy, Empire, and Victory.
>
> (4.570–78)

However, *Prometheus Unbound* is on the whole oracular and orphic rather than sublime. The exceptions, and they are important ones, occur mainly in acts 3 and 4, particularly the latter, where the motif of androgyny begins to take over in earnest. Throughout most of the first three acts Prometheus, representing the good genius of humankind, has been separated from his beloved Asia, who symbolizes (as Mary Shelley's note informs us) Nature, and also plays the part of what Blake would have called Prometheus's female emanation. Thus the situation is anti-androgynous in the extreme, and most of Prometheus's ejaculations in the first half of the play are masochistically "phallic."

As Demogorgon, who functions something like Blake's Spectre of Urthona, mentions in the drama's most crucial scene, "All things are subject [to Fate, Time, Occasion, Chance, and Change], but eternal Love" (2.3.120). This modifies considerably Demogorgon's famous enigmatic statement four lines earlier that "the deep truth is imageless." Ironically, Demogorgon is himself the product of the love of his father Jupiter for Thetis, as well as being the former's nemesis, so the concept of the deepest spring of all causality as an androgynous force, rather than a "face" or figure, is deeply embedded in the structure of the poem.

The most sublime portion of what constituted the original form of the drama—the first three acts—is the concluding speech of the Spirit of the Hour, describing the changes that have come over renovated human kind. As alert critics have noted, this speech tends to undercut itself rhetorically by being expressed mainly in terms of negatives:

> None wrought his lips in truth-entangling lines . . .
>
> (3.3.142)

> The loathsome mask has fallen, the man remains
> Sceptreless, free, uncircumscribed, but man

Equal, unclassed, tribeless, nationless.

                      (3.3.193–95)

An important exception to these perhaps unconsciously phallocentric negations is the prophetic vision of women's liberation contained within the same speech:

> And woman, too, frank, beautiful, and kind
> As the free heaven which rains fresh light and dew
> On the wide earth, past; gentle, radiant forms,
> From custom's evil taint exempt and pure;
> Speaking the wisdom once they could not think,
> Looking emotions once they feared to feel,
> And changed to all which once they dared not be,
> Yet being now, made earth like heaven.
>
>   (3.4.153–60)

Act 4, originally an afterthought, is conceived as a triumphal celebration of the delivered universe. Dramatically it has been called an anticlimax, coming as it does well after the unbinding of Prometheus, who doesn't appear in it. But this criticism is based on a misunderstanding of the poem's structure and overlooks the important point that the reason why Prometheus doesn't appear is that all the action is now taking place inside his androgynous mind. As the Chorus of Spirits sing, "We come from the mind / Of human kind" (4.93–94). The poem is a lyrical drama, and the finale is appropriately a choral hymn to the universal reign of love, containing some of Shelley's most sublime poetry in the androgynous mode. This includes Ione's vision (206–35) describing the chariot of the Moon, and Panthea's vision (236–318) describing the chariot of the Earth. Each chariot contains a sleeping child symbolic of cosmic renewal. Both speeches draw extensively on the visions of Ezekiel and the Book of Revelation: for instance, the "wingèd infant, white" (219) who sits within the former chariot, and the Spirit of the Earth in the latter, are both poetic conflations of the returned Christ and the Child of the Apocalypse.[7]

That the child *qua* child is androgynous is emphasized by Shelley's use of the pronoun *it* for both apocalyptic children. The same pronoun is used with reference to the Spirit of Love in Demogorgon's concluding speech:

> Love, from its awful throne of patient power
> In the wise heart, from the last giddy hour
>   Of dread endurance, from the slippery steep,

> And narrow verge of crag-like agony, springs
> And folds over the world its healing wings.

$$(4.557–61)$$

The aforementioned semantic difficulty pertaining to the relations between the sexes in the latter part of act 2 is now also, to a degree at least, overcome:

> Man, oh not men! a chain of linked thought,
> Of love and might to be divided not . . .
>
> Man, one harmonious soul of many a soul
> Whose nature is its own divine control.
> Where all things flow to all, as rivers to the sea;
> Familiar acts are beautiful through love;
> Labour, and pain, and grief, in life's green grove
> Sport like tame beasts, none knew how gentle they could be!

$$(4.394–405)$$

The delightful erotic speech of the Moon to the Earth, beginning "Thou art speeding round the sun / Brightest world of many a one" (4.457–58) shows not only that even such an elemental force as gravitational pull is humanized in Shelley's all-encompassing poetic vision, but also that, within the overall flexible androgynous context now envisaged, relative sexual differences can easily be accommodated, a point that is reinforced when the ecstatic Moon addresses her lover, the Earth, as "Brother" (4.476), reminding one of Shelley's earlier portrayal of Laon and Cythna.

Something similar happens in Shelley's major Platonic love poem *Epipsychidion,* arising out of his brief but intense infatuation with Emilia Viviani. Loosely based on the myth of Hyacinthus (a youth who was accidentally killed by his lover Apollo and was worshipped by the Spartans during an annual three-day festival that began by lamenting the death of Hyacinthus and ended by celebrating Apollo) the poem begins as allegorical erotic autobiography of a sort that has set some readers' teeth on edge. However, Shelley ascends the Platonic ladder until, in the last two hundred lines, the poem reaches rare heights of androgynous (rather than merely erotic) vision:

> Emily,
> A ship is floating in the harbour now,
> A wind is hovering o'er the mountain's brow;

> There is a path on the sea's azure floor,
> No keel has ever plowed that path before;
> The halcyons brood around the foamless isles;
> The treacherous Ocean has foresworn its wiles;
> The merry mariners are bold and free:
> Say, my heart's sister, wilt thou sail with me?
>
> (407–15)

From here on, Emily becomes still more rarefied until she is wholly symbolic, like Dante's Beatrice or Blake's Jerusalem, as the multiple references to the myth of the Golden Age attest.[8] An important aspect of this mythopoeic process is Shelley's renewed interest in prelapsarian incest-cum-androgyny:

> but, for delight,
> Some wise and tender Ocean-King, ere crime
> Had been invented, in the world's young prime,
> Reared . . . a pleasure-house
> Made sacred to his sister and his spouse.
>
> (487–92)

The central relationship recalls that of the Song of Songs, just as Shelley's "pleasure-house" recalls the pleasure-dome in Coleridge's "Kubla Khan," so that what is prelapsarian becomes postlapsarian when androgynized by the alchemy of poetic genius:

> The fountains of our deepest life, shall be
> Confused in Passion's golden purity,
> As mountain-springs under the morning sun.
> We shall become the same, we shall be one,
> Spirit within two frames, Oh! wherefore two?
>
> (570–74)

Shelley wants not merely "one Spirit" but one frame, which he now realizes can be attained, if at all, only through death:

> one life, one death,
> One Heaven, one Hell, one immortality,
> And one annihilation.
>
> (585–87)

The following half line—"Woe is me!"—echoes the dying words of Hyacinthus referred to earlier (69), thus resolving the existential dilemma into the realm of myth and ritual. The death of the ego (Hyacinthus) gives way to the celebration of poetry (Apollo, who killed what he loved and made it immortal). It is perhaps more than a coincidence that this poem was substantially completed by Saint Valentine's Day, 1821. A few months earlier Shelley had handled a similar theme with greater objectivity and mythopoetic wit, perhaps with an assist from Mary.

"Song of Apollo" and "Song of Pan" were written by Shelley in 1820 for inclusion in Mary's mythological drama *Midas,* based on the account of a poetical contest in Ovid's *Metamorphoses.* In Ovid's version Pan sings first and Apollo overcomes him; Mary (who retitled Shelley's songs "hymns") reverses the order, giving Pan the last word.[9]

Shelley's poems, each thirty-six lines long, present a study in stylistic contrast. "Song of Apollo" impresses with its static structure—six six-line stanzas of rhyming iambic pentameter—and is a parody of the egotistical or "phallic" sublime. The pronoun *I* is used ten times, most devastatingly in the opening of the last stanza: "I am the eye with which the Universe / Beholds itself, and knows it is divine" (31–32). In "Song of Pan" Shelley further subverts Ovid's account by tilting the balance in favor of Pan, who, in contrast to Apollo's egotism, begins by using the first-person plural, with a hint of androgyny: "From the forests and highlands / We come, we come" (1–2). Pan's song has an intricate and "romantic" twelve-line stanza, with lines of varying length in which the number of syllables also varies, from four to eleven per line, as in Coleridge's "Christabel." Whereas Apollo's song, with its rigidly controlled order, appears imposed from above, Pan's "sweet pipings" seem to warble up from below, enchanting the waves, the "wind in the reeds and the rushes," the bees and birds, as well as the cicadae and lizards (st. 1). In the second stanza Pan's song is said to have rendered the "sileni and sylvans and fauns" as well as the sea and wood nymphs silent with love: "as you now, Apollo, / For envy of my sweet pipings" (23–24).* In the last stanza Pan sings of the creation, including the "dancing stars," the "daedal Earth," and the "giant wars," modulating this into a poignant lament for his lost love Syrinx, who, after being changed into a reed, upon which Pan says he was impaled, became fashioned into the pan-pipes, symbolizing the androgyny of art.

The repetition of "envy," this time attributed to both Apollo

---

*Since Ovid does not mention Apollo's envy of Pan, Shelley, who clearly identifies with the latter, may be conflating this myth with that of the flayed Marsyas, whose flute-playing overcame Apollo's lyre, as a type of the crucified artist.

(Byron?) and Tmolus (Mary?), who unlike the others are unable to weep "At the sorrow of [Pan's] sweet pipings" (34–36), introduces a theme that permeates Shelley's later lyrics: the identification of artistic creation through suffering with the maternal experience of physical birthing.[10] Seen from this perspective, all art is doubly androgynous, since the mind or soul is "masculine" in relation to the body, but "feminine" in relation to God, or the creative and destructive power of Love.

"The Witch of Atlas": Shelley's "intensest rime"

One of Shelley's least read and most widely misunderstood poems, "The Witch of Atlas" deals in an apparently playful manner with the story of a witch who creates a hermaphrodite as her companion. Shelley had translated Plato's *Symposium,* including Aristophanes' speech about the androgyne, while at the Bagni di Lucca, and was particularly interested in seeing a statue of a sleeping hermaphrodite in Rome's Palazzo Borghese.[11]

When Shelley wrote "The Witch of Atlas," 14–16 August 1820, he had his major work *Prometheus Unbound* behind him and was able to indulge himself in what has been unfairly dismissed as "this light-weight virtuoso piece."[12] The circumstances of the poem's composition were propitious: Shelley conceived it during a solitary weekend pilgrimage he had been planning for two years to Monte San Pelegrino, above Lucca in the Tuscan sub-Apennines, during which he climbed to a little chapel on the peak of the mountain, itself a synthesis of female and male symbolism. Returning home exhausted from his climb—the weather was hot—Shelley began work on his "Witch" on Monday morning, and completed it two days later. Mary notes in her journal that the remarkable rapidity of the poem's composition—more than 200 lines a day—is unmatched by any of Shelley's other works.

Unpublished during Shelley's lifetime, "The Witch of Atlas" first appeared in his *Posthumous Poems,* edited by his widow. In the dedication, "To Mary, on her objecting to the following poem, upon the score of its containing no human interest," Shelley at once blames and forgives her for having allowed herself to become "critic-bitten" to the extent of complaining that the poem "tell[s] no story" (1–4). He also lightly (and rightly) boasts about the rapid composition of this, his pet poem, comparing it favourably to Wordsworth's "Peter Bell":

> Though he took nineteen years, and she three days
> In dressing. Light the vest of flowing metre

> She wears; he, proud as dandy with his stays,
> Has hung upon his wiry limbs a dress
> Like King Lear's 'looped and windowed raggedness.'
>
> (36–40)

The references to "dressing," "vest," and "stays," in conjunction
with male and female characters, remind one of the motif of cross-
dressing and disguise that we have encountered in our discussion
of Byron's *Don Juan,* a motif Shelley again alludes to at the end
of his dedication:

> If you unveil my Witch, no priest nor primate
> Can shrive you of that sin—if sin there be
> In love, when it becomes idolatry.
>
> (45–47)

Here Shelley is looking beyond Mary to posterity and daring the
critics to do their worst: what follows is a poet's poem considerably
in advance of its time. The daring abandonment of narrative as a
significant structural principle invites comparison with Byron's
still-undervalued *Beppo,* as well as Blake's *Jerusalem* and Joyce's
Finnegans Wake; the first and last of these three works share some
of "The Witch's" deceptively playful exterior.

The poem's playfulness is reflected in the deft use of the ottava
rima stanza that Byron was concurrently using in *Don Juan,* a
similarity that is also reflected in the occasional burlesques of
Wordsworth and the use of such atypical (for Shelley) images as
"bats at the wired window of a dairy" (173). Shelley's eldritch
sense of humor, held in check in his more "serious" poems, is
given free reign here, as in "Peter Bell the Third," his devastating
parody of Wordsworth, and in the laughing paradoxes of "The
Cloud."

Shelley begins by telling us that the lady Witch, a daughter of
Apollo, lived in a cave on Mount Atlas before the end of the Saturnian Golden Age. Like that other mysterious lady in Shelley's
Neoplatonic allegory of the same period, "The Sensitive Plant," the
Witch has no consort, but she too is endowed with the necessary
narcissism of the artist, and creates for herself a beautiful winged
creature whom she playfully calls "Hermaphroditus" (388), after
the bisexual child of Hermes and Aphrodite. That this designation
is not meant to be taken literally is indicated by the following
stanza:

A sexless thing it was, and in its growth
   It seemed to have developed no defect
Of either sex, yet all the grace of both,—
   In gentleness and strength its limbs were decked;
The bosom swelled lightly with its full youth,
   The countenance was such as might select
Some artist that his skill should never die,
Imaging forth such perfect purity.

(329–36)

The Witch and her creature are really less "sexless" (329; 589) than androgynous: Shelley is using a poetic variation of Plato's myth of the androgyne to prophesy a restoration of the Golden Age:

Her cave was stored with scrolls of strange device,
   The works of some Saturnian Archimage,
Which taught the expiations at whose price
   Men from the Gods might win that happy age
Too lightly lost, redeeming native vice;
   And which might quench the Earth-consuming rage
Of gold and blood—till men should live and move
Harmonious as the sacred stars above.

(185–92)

This transformation is to be effected by means of a synthesis of the manners and motifs of androgyny and (paradoxically) sexual fulfilment, with the former guiding the latter and transmuting it through what Blake had called "an improvement of sensual enjoyment" into a superior androgynous condition:

And timid lovers who had been so coy,
   They hardly knew whether they loved or not,
Would rise out of their rest, and take sweet joy,
   To the fulfilment of their inmost thought;
And when next day the maiden and the boy
   Met one another, both like sinners caught,
Blushed at the thing which each believed was done
Only in fancy—till the tenth moon shone;

And then the Witch would let them take no ill:
   Of many thousand schemes which lovers find,
The Witch found one,—and so they took their fill
   Of happiness in marriage warm and kind.
Friends who, by practice of some envious skill,
   Were torn apart—a wide wound, mind from mind!—

> She did unite again with visions clear
> Of deep affections and of truth sincere.
>
> (649–64)

Shelley's aforementioned reference to the Witch and her companion as "sexless" reminds one of a significant difference of emphasis from the norm in his translation of the *Symposium:*

> First, then, human beings were formerly not divided into two sexes, male and female; there was also a third, common to both the others, the name of which remains, though the sex itself has disappeared. *The androgynous sex, both in appearance and in name, was common to both male and female; its name alone remains, which labours under a reproach.*[13]

Shelley is suggesting, here as in "The Witch," the paradox that a given character may at once be "androgynous" and retain something of his or her masculine or feminine identity. In Plato, the primordial androgynes were split up into heterosexual men and women, while primordial males and females were split up into gay males and lesbians.

Something similar is intimated in a certain Biblical passages of which Shelley would have been aware:

> For when they shall rise from the dead,
> they neither marry, nor are given in marriage;
> but are as the angels which are in heaven.
>
> (Mark 12:25)

> There is neither Jew nor Greek, there is neither bond
> nor free, there is neither male nor female; for ye are
> all one in Christ Jesus.
>
> (Gal. 3:28)

Whether or not "The Witch of Atlas" is sublime in the androgynous sense—it undoubtedly subverts more traditional notions of sublimity—is a moot question. Certainly this "intensest rime" (to borrow a self-reflexive pun buried in the poem's text, line 399) has challenged its critics, one of whom refers to the poem, in a rather interesting reversal of the usual relations between poetry and criticism, as "a threat to coherent interpretation."[14] It is also a light-hearted reply to Mary Shelley's *Frankenstein,* whose motif of failed androgyny it effectively reverses. Like the winged creature who becomes the poem's inner symbol, "The Witch of Atlas" may perhaps best be regarded as a sublime artifice centered on the motif of androgyny, anticipating (and no doubt influencing) Yeats's Byzantine and other visions.[15]

The Sublime Androgyny of *Adonais*

Although Shelley's androgynous quest culminated in the playful polymorphous perversity of "The Witch of Atlas," he was to have one more go at the theme in *Adonais,* his great pastoral elegy on the death of John Keats, wherein myth and ritual again figure prominently. Since much of this poem concerns the poetic achievement and character of Keats, to be considered in the following chapter, I shall here confine myself to a few observations on the set piece near the middle of the poem, which is sometimes referred to as Shelley's narcissistic self-portrait (st. 31–34), and the conclusion.

But first, a brief detour. We have noticed in discussing "Alastor" that narcissism is androgyny *manqué.* It may well also be a necessary part of a certain type of creative personality, insofar as the myth of Narcissus beautifully symbolizes a type of self-absorption that Shelley refers to throughout his poetry. Sometimes he dovetails this to the motif of androgyny, as in "The Sensitive Plant," where the narcissi are called "the fairest among . . . all" (18) the flowers in a garden tended by a companionless Lady and featuring a type of mimosa whose androgyny mirrors hers, whatever botanists might say.

In what amounts to his valedictory self-portrait in *Adonais,* Shelley refers to himself as "frail" and "companionless" (271–72), like the Sensitive Plant (12). He also describes himself as "A pardlike Spirit beautiful and swift" (280), reminding one that the adjective "beautiful" was conspicuously withheld from his description of the Sensitive Plant:

> For the Sensitive Plant has no bright flower;
> Radiance and odour are not its dower;
> It loves, even like Love, its deep heart is full,
> It desires what it has not, the Beautiful!
>
> (74–77)

When he wrote "The Sensitive Plant" (which predates "The Witch of Atlas" by a few months), Shelley saw himself as an androgyne *manqué,* poetically unfulfilled, the miracle of *Prometheus Unbound* notwithstanding. In *Adonais,* which he came to regard as his "least imperfect" and "most highly wrought" work of art—his *chef d'oeuvre,* in other words—Shelley seems to have scrupulously followed the dying Keats's advice to "be more of an artist and load every rift of your subject with ore."[16] If so, then the set piece containing Shelley's self-portrait may have been inserted late in the poem's composition, perhaps as a sort of afterthought or signature, in the manner of certain Renaissance artists. Needless to say, this possibility makes the passage in question all the more interesting. Shelley, with a double assist from Keats, has now attained "the Beautiful," both in the highly wrought artistry of *Adonais* and in the concomitant self-love and self-acceptance that enable him to face his own tragic destiny. Acteon-like, he has "gazed on Nature's naked loveliness" (275) and paid the price; hence he is one "[w]ho in another's fate now wept his own" (300), fatally wounded by the critics' darts, and thus able to portray the poetic truth of Keats's fate with empathy and sincerity.

Shelley also portrays himself as something of an androgyne;

> His head was bound with pansies overblown,
> And faded violets, white, and pied, and blue;
> And a light spear topped with a cypress cone,
> Round whose rude shaft dark ivy-tresses grew
> Yet dripping with the forest's noonday dew,
> Vibrated, as the ever-beating heart
> Shook the weak hand that grasped it.

> (289–95)

The synthesis of feminine and masculine images and symbols is quite deliberate, modulating from the floral garlands around Shelley's head to the phallic and Dionysian "spear topped with a cypress cone," the "rude shaft" of the thyrsus testifying to the "manlier" aspects of Shelley's personality, including a keen interest in and appreciation of the pleasures of sensual love: qualities that he had in common with Keats. But Dionysus, or Bacchus, called twice-born because after his original birth he was sewn in his father Zeus's thigh till he reached maturity, was also sometimes portrayed as an androgyne and had prophetic powers.

Shelley's androgynous self-portrait serves a functional purpose in that it helps to define the dual character of the romantic poet-as-artist, with the last lines of the set piece establishing Shelley's identity—and by implication that of Keats—as one of those whom Blake characterizes in *Milton* as the prophetic reprobate:

> sad Urania scanned
> The Stranger's mien, and murmured: 'Who art thou?'

He answered not, but with a sudden hand
Made bare his branded and ensanguined brow,
Which was like Cain's or Christ's—oh! that it should be so!

(302–6)

Destroyer and preserver, Shelley now recognizes in himself the doubly dual nature of the androgynous artist, which the gentler Keats had also, to a degree, shared, arousing the envy of (among others) Byron by daring to write so well and die so young.

This concept of the artist as androgyne also underlies the sublime coda of *Adonais,* which has been called "a metaphysical defence of suicide,"[17] but is really an intensification of the aforementioned idea of the prophetic reprobate in which creative artists are identified with the crucified Christ:

The breath whose might I have invoked in song
Descends on me; my spirit's bark is driven,
Far from the shore, far from the trembling throng
Whose sails were never to the tempest given;
The massy earth and spheréd skies are riven!
I am borne darkly, fearfully, afar;
Whilst, burning through the inmost veil of Heaven,
The soul of Adonais, like a star,
Beacons from the abode where the Eternal are.

(487–95)

Suffering implies androgyny because of the metaphorical nexus of creativity and giving birth (as well as dying), which is picked up in the pun on "borne" in line 492; "fearfully," in the same line, shows Shelley being not afraid to reveal "unmasculine" emotions, another indication of androgyny. Likewise, martyrdom to one's vision holds the promise of supreme androgynous fulfilment: "No more let Life divide what Death can join together" (476). The references to "the massy earth and spheréd skies" being "riven," and to the "veil of Heaven" in the final stanza echo Luke, 24:45, and also remind one that Blake refers in *Jerusalem* (55:16) to the veil of Vala or Nature as "a veil the Saviour born and dying rends," likewise succinctly identifying sex, birth, death, and (androgynous) rebirth. That Shelley could not have known *Jerusalem* helps to establish the autonomy of his vision, as well as the archetypal quality of the symbolism involved. To the end, he was the enchanted androgyne.

6

Keats's Immortal Androgyny

Keats's Androgynous Poetical Character

WILLIAM HAZLITT, IN AN ESSAY ENTITLED "ON EFFEMINACY OF Character" (1822), declares his esteem for "a manly firmness of decision," and discusses Keats's work as an example of "effeminacy of style, in some degree corresponding to an effeminacy of character."[1] Hazlitt, who prided himself upon what the Victorian writer Mary Coleridge called his "downright cut-and-thrust manliness"[2] of style, is here expressing what has until recently been the conventional view of Keats. Even Keats, contrasting himself to his most famous poetic contemporary, felt constrained to admit that "Lord Byron cuts a figure"—although he adds cuttingly, "but he is not figurative"—in contrast to both "the wordsworthian [sic] or egotistical sublime" and Keats's articulation of his own type of "poetical character": a "camelion," with "no self . . . no identity," and by implication at least no distinct gender, insofar as the poetical character takes "as much delight in conceiving an Iago as an Imogen."[3] Hazlitt is of course being unfair to Keats, as Keats is to Byron, which is to say both oversimplify. (Byron thought he was being "true to Nature in making the [sexual] advances come from the females" in *Don Juan,* and several critics, among them Northrop Frye, have remarked on Juan's "passivity," perhaps exaggerating it.[4])

In certain respects Keats's poetic career, beginning with his portrayal of powerful females dominating young males (e.g., Cynthia and Endymion, Isabella and Lorenzo) and proceeding to such works as the "heroic" *Hyperion,* which impressed even Byron, and the crisp couplets of *Lamia,* reads like an inversion of Byron's. True, Lamia dominates Lycius: but Keats condemns this relationship, both through the use of irony, and also more explicitly through the words of Apollonius, who calls Lycius a triple fool just before his death. Moreover, Keats's remarkable early sonnet

116

"On First Looking Into Chapman's Homer" has often been cited for its manly boldness of conception and execution. In it, Keats not only "cuts a figure," but is also figurative.[5]

Susan Wolfson, in an article on *Don Juan* I have referred to earlier, remarks on "how slippery such distinctions [as Hazlitt's] become as soon as one applies pressure," and observes that Lady Blessington found Byron towards the end of his life "a perfect chameleon" who "take the colour of whatever touches him . . . owing to the extreme *mobilité* of his nature." Of Keats, Wolfson observes that his verse tales and letters "are in many ways the reflex of a sexism that is hostile, adolescent, and more deeply entrenched than Byron's for want of intimate friendships with women that complicate Byron's attitudes."[6] Now Keats's conception of the poetical character is, as we have seen, androgynous. If Wolfson is right—as I suspect she is, at least in part—about the "reflex" of an adolescent sexism in Keats's poetry, it might be a worthwhile enterprise to try and refine the Keatsian poetical character by separating it, where possible, from the dross of such "sexism," which may well be (as Wolfson intimates) primarily the attitudinal reflex of ungratified desire.

To revert briefly to "On First Looking Into Chapman's Homer" (1816), Keats's first fully accomplished poem: I have referred to its "manly boldness," but this is itself a figure of speech. At least as important is the way the sonnet anticipates Keats's later concept of "half knowledge," or doctrine of negative capability, an aspect of what we have been calling poetic androgyny:

> I mean Negative Capability, that is when a man is capable of being in uncertainties, Mysteries, doubts, without any irritable reaching after fact & reason—Coleridge, for instance, would let go by a fine isolated verisimilitude caught from the Penetralium of mystery, from being incapable of remaining content with half knowledge.[7]

It is perhaps worth noting that in this letter written in December 1818, Keats is referring to the later Coleridge, who had declined from poetry into metaphysics and criticism. As for the aforementioned sonnet, it could hardly have been written as we know it if Keats had not been ignorant of Greek—something he also adverts to in his later sonnet "To Homer": "Standing aloof in giant ignorance / Of thee I hear and of the Cyclades" (1–2).[8] The most profound line of this poem, "Aye on the shores of darkness there is light," suggests a kind of yin-yang concept of existence with feminine and masculine powers equally balanced, as does the oxymoronic analogy between Homer's physical blindness and Keats's "giant ignorance" of Greek on the one hand, and the "triple sight" that he ascribes not only to Homer (and, by implication, himself), but also, in the last line, "To Dian, Queen of Earth, and Heaven, and Hell."

This somewhat "oriental" and detached concept of sexual balance also underlies Keats's deft handling of the loves of Cupid and Psyche and the rest in the latter part of "I Stood Tip-Toe" (1816), a sort of trial run for some of his later and greater mythopoeia. It is perhaps worth noting that in contradistinction to Shelley, whose "Alastor" had appeared a year earlier, and for whom the myth of Echo and Narcissus was to become something of an obsession, Keats goes out of his way to detach himself from Narcissus by implicitly contrasting him with the eponymous "forlorn flower, with naught of pride" (172), the sight of which presumably inspired some long-forgotten poet to create the original myth. We have observed that Narcissism is androgyny *manqué;* evidently the early Keats, whatever his other psychological shortcomings may have been, was more on guard against this solipsistic tendency than either Byron or Shelley.

Central to Keats's sense of poetic vocation is a strange vision he had, apparently during a sleepless night spent in Leigh Hunt's study in November 1817 when he conceived "Sleep and Poetry." The account of this remarkable vision comprises some fifty lines in the poem that tell of a chariot descending from heaven to earth, beginning with the exclamation "for lo! I see afar / O'er sailing the blue cragginess, a car" (125–26), and going on to dramatize the divine origin of poetry in terms that are at once mythic, mysterious, and implicitly androgynous:

> The charioteer with wond'rous gesture talks
> To the trees and mountains; and there soon appear
> Shapes of delight, of mystery, and fear,
> Passing along before a dusky space
> Made by some mighty oaks: as they would chase
> Some ever-fleeting music, on they sweep.
> Lo! *how they murmur, laugh, and smile, and weep:*
> Some with upholden hand and mouth severe;
> Some with their faces muffled to the ear
> Between their arms; *some, clear in youthful bloom,*
> Go glad and smilingly athwart the gloom.
> (136–46; emphasis added)

These angels, extraterrestrials, or whatever they are, number in the "thousands," are able to appear in "different ways" (148), involve some sexual differentiation (149, 154) combined with an overall impression of androgyny, and are endowed with "broad wings" (151), such as those Keats had aspired to see his own shoulders sprout earlier (81–84) in the poem. They have come to give Keats a conception of his life's work, as he realizes once "The visions are all fled," when he remarks:

> I will strive
> Against all doubtings, and will keep alive
> The thought of that same chariot, and the strange
> Journey it went.

(155–62)

The passage as a whole not only invites comparison and contrast with Wordsworth's solitary experience of near-mystical dedication to poetry, which also followed a sleepless night, as described in the not-yet-published *Prelude* (4.309–38), but—more germane to the present study—may also be contrasted to the patriarchal-sounding "huge and mighty forms, that do not live / Like living men" (*Prelude,* 1.398–99) that haunted Wordsworth's childhood. Clearly, the evolving Keatsian sublime as represented by this remarkable passage is not only less egotistical, but more androgynous than that of his great predecessor.

Keats's androgynous poetical character is reflected throughout his early poems, such as the sonnet "After Dark Vapours," which builds up to one of several prophetic anticipations of his untimely death and includes a parallel reference to "Sweet Sappho" (12), his feminine counterpart. Another sonnet of this period, "On the Sea," notable for its use of synaesthetic imagery ("shadowy sound" [4], "cloying melody" [12]) more subtly illustrates the point that poets are fond of such rhetorical devices as synaesthesia and oxymoron because they are metaphors for androgyny insofar as they too reconcile apparent opposites.

The same applies, as we have noticed in our discussion of Byron and Shelley, to the use of the incest motif. This may be seen in displaced form in Keats's first long poem, *Endymion*. Endymion is the first in a succession of Apollonian heroes in Keats's poetry. His feminine counterparts in the poem—Diana the moon-goddess, Endymion's sister Peona, and the Indian Maid, the last of whom appears in book 4 and ultimately reveals herself as Diana—are really all aspects of one being, sometimes known as the triple goddess, to whom Keats referred at the end of his sonnet "To Homer." They are also aspects of something inside Endymion's own nature, or something required for the completion of that nature, which is why the poem is full of metaphors combining creativity and procreation, such as the phrase "a new birth" (1.297)—this phrase also occurs in Shelley's "Ode to the West Wind" (64)—references to sleep and dreams as the key to the unconscious mind (1.453–65), womb and cavern imagery, and so forth.

The famous "Pleasure Thermometer" passage (1.769–842)—an ingenious variation on the theme of the Platonic ladder—develops what is essentially a sacramental conception of "love and friendship," according to which "our souls interknit / So wingedly" as to regain something of their original androgynous unity. The passage continues,

> when we combine therewith,
> Life's self is nourish'd by its proper pith,
> And we are nurtured like a pelican brood.
>
> (1.801–15)

The pelican was fabled to feed its young with blood from its own breast, an enterprise in which both parents were ultimately involved (s.v. "Pelican," *Encycl. Brit.*, 11th ed.). This has given the pelican an important place in ecclesiastical heraldry, and the bird's ovoid shape may also recall Plato's myth of the egg-shaped androgyne, since Keats, like most of the romantics, was interested in combining Christian and classical mythology.

As aforementioned, Endymion is an Apollonian hero, an aspiring Phoebus looking for his Phoebe. (Phoebus-Apollo and Phoebe, or Diana, were of course twin brother and sister—another androgynous metaphor.) Essentially the same pattern underlies Keats's later romances "Isabella, or the Pot or Basil" and "The Eve of St. Agnes."[9] Each of these poems accordingly has an androgynous aspect, based on the pattern established in *Endymion,* but with certain significant variations. Isabella, after her lover is murdered, passes through two stages, the first of which is merely narcissistic grief (233–40), androgyny *manqué*. The second stage, beginning with Isabella's dream-vision of the dead Lorenzo and proceeding to her discovery, exhumation, and decapitation of his corpse, involves the incorporation by her of aspects of his more "masculine" nature, such as courage and resolve, which is why she says at one point, "Sweet Spirit, thou hast school'd my infancy" (334), albeit she is eventually driven mad by her patriarchal brothers.

In "The Eve of St. Agnes," the turning point similarly comes when the awakened becomes the awakener, the "ravished" the rav-

isher, and Madeline bids Porphyro arise from the deathlike state
as he kneels by her bed—"pallid, chill, and drear!" (311)—to consummate their love and fulfill the legend as well as the myth. After
the consummation, which involves an essentially androgynous apotheosis, Porphyro exclaims:

> "My Madeline! sweet dreamer! lovely bride!
> Say, May I be for aye thy vassal blest?
> Thy beauty's shield, heart-shap'd and vermeil dyed?"
>
> (334–36)

The vermilion coloration of the heart-shaped shield reminds one
of the "pelican brood" passage in Endymion (some pelicans have
rose or salmon-colored plumage), and the image once more reso-
nates with Plato's ovoid androgyne. The lovers' counterparts in
the poem, old Angela and the Beadsman, both of whom are essentially self-sacrificing and die at the end, represent the old life that
is being cast off, as though it were the eggshell or cocoon from
which the new society symbolized by Madeline and Porphyro,
which will incorporate aspects of the old, has sprung. This helps
to round out the pattern of androgynous unity.

Unlike the supple style of "The Eve of St. Agnes," which unrolls
like a medieval tapestry, on the whole the style of Hyperion—
begun late in 1818, shortly before "The Eve of St. Agnes," and
abandoned not long thereafter—is not sublime in the androgynous
sense, though it may well be sublime in more traditional ways.
Keats was at this time struggling to assimilate the diverse influ-
ences of Milton and Wordsworth, and the result, though certainly
impressive, now appears to have been something of an anachro-
nism, as Keats himself was quick to realize, claiming that there
were "too many Miltonic inversions in it."[10] As Morris Dickstein
remarks, "there is a tension between the abstractness and imper-
sonality of the form and the actuality of the content."[11]

The theme of Hyperion, on the other hand, best epitomized in
the great and somewhat supple speech of Oceanus in book 2, does
have androgynous implications. This theme is essentially that the
gods, as well as nature, are subject to change:

> "We fall by course of Nature's law, not force
> Of thunder, or of Jove . . .
>   for 'tis the eternal law
> That first in beauty should be first in might."
>
> (2.181–229)

The articulation of this theme by the more yielding Oceanus, in contrast to the blustering rhetoric of Hyperion, enables the former to take vicarious pleasure in the beauty and perfection of his successor, Neptune:

> "Have ye beheld the young God of the Sea,
> My dispossessor? Have ye seen his face?
> Have ye beheld his chariot, foam'd along
> By noble winged creatures he hath made?
> I saw him on the calmed waters scud,
> With such a glow of beauty in his eyes,
> That it enforc'd me to bid sad farewell
> To all my empire: farewell sad I look,
> And hither came, to see how dolorous fate
> Had wrought upon ye; and how I might best
> Give consolation in this woe extreme.
> Receive the truth, and let it be your balm."
>
> (2.232–43)

One is reminded of a university professor facing retirement and clearing out his office before turning it over to a young man or (more likely) woman who has just been granted tenure.

Oceanus's speech, as I have observed elsewhere, also represents an aspect of Keatsian "disinterestedness" or negative capability, which we have seen to be intrinsically androgynous. Oceanus and his daughter Clymene, whose speech follows his and goes on to comprehend the birth of Apollo (successor to Hyperion and founder of poetry), play a role in the fragment somewhat like that of the Beadsman and the Beldame in "The Eve of St. Agnes," except that the former pair are thematically more important as well as more explicitly androgynous. Thus Oceanus's reference to his "locks not oozy" (2.170)—so described because he has been dispossessed from his native element—presents a parallel with a difference to the "dewy locks" of the androgynous Savior of Blake's "To Spring." Oceanus's description of the "dull soil" feeding the comely "forest-trees" (2.217–24) also reminds one of Blake's *Book of Thel* and "The Clod and the Pebble," particularly the former, with its protagonist who resisted change to her own spiritual detriment, in contrast to the sublime disinterestedness of Oceanus and Clymene.

The fragment breaks off early in book 3 with an account of Apollo apparently about to assume his godhead (die into life) and emitting a shriek that presents another intriguing parallel with *The Book of Thel*, this time with Thel's shriek, which likewise comes in the penultimate line. Both passages, ironically or otherwise, turn upon what we have seen to be the central metaphor of sublime androgyny: the imaginative identity of childbirth and creativity. One is also reminded of the famous Shelleyan shriek, in a passage that Keats would have read ("Hymn to Intellectual Beauty," line 60), on whose androgynous implications I remarked earlier. Perhaps in Shelley, and in Keats's Apollo, Thel is shrieking back into life.

Morris Dickstein has observed that "the Keats of the odes is a different poet," and he attributes this qualitative change to "the metamorphosis of Apollo in the third book of *Hyperion*," as well as to Keats's discovery of what Dickstein refers to as the "quasi-ironic" style of "The Eve of St. Agnes":

The sensuous Apollo must die into life, must be convulsed by "knowledge enormous," as the "creations and destroyings" of human history are proved upon his pulses. Conversely, the lovers in *The Eve of St. Agnes*, . . . their very motives hedged by the poet's near ironies, can only escape into myth and legend.[12]

There are two contrary impulses here, toward tragic involvement and toward ironic detachment, which is why Dickstein says the odes are "built on a conception of the imagination which is dialectical and tragic rather than escapist."[13] While agreeing in essence with this estimate, I tend to see Keats's involvement, though leavened by playful irony, as uppermost in the odes, with the ironic mode clarifying itself in *Lamia,* and a near-miraculous equipoise being finally attained in the serene involved detachment of "To Autumn."

To relate this broad pattern of development to the mode and motif of the androgynous sublime is not too difficult as far as either part of the equation is concerned. "Ode to Psyche," in its style and content, is one of the most androgynous poems ever written, portraying as it does the love of a goddess who is also the human mind or soul and a winged boy who resembles a more overtly erotic version of Hermaphroditus in Shelley's "The Witch of Atlas." The function of this enchanted couple—rather like that of Shelley's Witch and her companion—is to open the windows of the body-soul continuum and "let the warm Love in!" (67).

Stylistically the poem is remarkable for its use of oxymoron and synaesthesia—"fragrant-eyed" (13), "delicious moan" (30), "fond believing lyre" (a kind of triple oxymoron, line 37), "pleasant pain" (52)—which are rhetorical devices we have seen to be metaphors for androgyny. Thus the allegory of poetic androgyny characterizes both the poem's theme, with its powerful internalizing pull according to which a beautiful goddess becomes the (male) poet's mind, and a style of opposites harmoniously combined. Hence the poem's playful irony: psyche is praising Psyche, eros Eros.

In "Ode to a Nightingale" the primary symbol of poetic androgyny is the nightingale itself. Keats quickly moves from the drowsy, gustatory imagery of the self-involved opening lines ("My heart aches . . . as though of hemlock I had drunk, / Or emptied some dull opiate") to his oxymoronic objective correlative, the "happy" bird, who "Singest of summer with full-throated ease." The nightingale thus becomes at once the sensuous poet (the cock alone sings, as part of its mating ritual) and a "light winged Dryad" or wood-nymph, combining from the outset characteristics of both sexes (1–10).

The sexually tinged synaesthesia of the second stanza ("O for a draught of vintage . . . / Tasting of Flora and the country green") reinforces the androgynous motif, as does the personification of the wine-beaker "With beaded bubbles winking at the brim / And purple-stained mouth," an artful conflation of a perhaps still-randy Silenus and a (feminine) wine goblet. The buried reference to the Silenoi—fat, drunken old men who followed Bacchus and were probably past it sexually—not only subtly reinforces the androgynous implications of this stanza, but also anticipates the countermovement of the next one, with its antithetical allusions to the death of Keats's brother Tom and the old men he had seen in the wards of London hospitals: the negative androgyny of sickness, old age, and death.

Bacchus and his pards are rejected in the fourth stanza in favor of "the viewless wings of Poesy," whereupon, beginning with the exclamation "Already with thee!" Keats suddenly *becomes* the nightingale of his imagination in sixteen remarkable lines (35–50) that are among the most empathetic in English poetry. All the poet's senses are open, with the partial exception of sight ("But here there is no light, / Save what from heaven is with the breezes blown"), as women were formerly supposed to close their eyes while making love: hence, the implied androgyny of the *partial* darkness here.

After the transcendent moment of imaginative union is over, the womb-tomb imagery of "embalmed darkness" gives way with a kind of tragic inevitability to Keats's expression of the deathwish, though this too is hedged about with ironic ambiguity:

I *have been half in love* with *easeful Death* . . .
Now more than ever *seems* it *rich to die,*
To cease upon the midnight *with no pain.*

(52–56, emphasis added).

One is reminded of Shakespeare's Cleopatra, of whom Octavius remarked, "She hath pursued conclusions infinite / Of easy ways to die" (5.358–59).

The easy out of a painless death was not for Keats, however. The poem remains true to is androgynous poetical character by following an alternating rhythm of "escape" or withdrawal and return with renewed intensity. The latter is most memorably portrayed in the famous penultimate stanza, where Keats's thrusting defiance at the prospect of a death he knew to be imminent powerfully pulls the poem together again: "Thou wast not born for death, immortal Bird!" Poetry, here symbolized by what Keats elsewhere calls "the poetry of earth,"[14] alone involves birth without the tragic closure of death: hence it is immortally androgynous. "Emperor and clown" combine social opposites among those who have heard the nightingale's song; the superb description of Ruth—an ancestress of Jesus whom Keats elsewhere described as "a deep one"[15]—remembering it in her "sad heart" as she "stood in tears amid the alien corn" not only restores the gender side of the equation, but also gives us an unforgettable image of the androgynous poet (including whoever wrote the Book of Ruth) as an alien in this world, longing for the fulfilment of absolute return.

Whereas "Ode to a Nightingale" begins with a statement and ends with two questions, "Ode on a Grecian Urn" reverses the process, beginning with a series of questions and concluding with a famous affirmation whose reverberations are still being felt in critical circles. Related to this note of greater certainty is the way in which the urn with its womblike shape becomes a symbol of Sophia, the Bride of Wisdom mentioned in the Book of Proverbs in whom God's creation was mirrored or conceived.[16] The urn is described as "still unravished" at the outset because Sophia is always referred to as a virgin, and God's creation of the world out of his heavenly Wisdom (as interpreted by Boehme) was in effect the original Virgin Birth.[17] Indeed, it is possible to imagine a mystical marriage of form and content, of time and eternity, taking place while the poem is read, with the climax or consummation coming with the six-times repeated "happy" in the central stanza.[18]

According to this interpretation it is the urn as Sophia who speaks the wise words of the concluding couplet, affirming the

supreme identity of Beauty and Truth, which—like all wise say-
ings—is meant only for the initiate. Buddha, writing out of a different tradition, affirmed that which is good is always beautiful, but
that which is beautiful is not always good.[19] However, Keats is not
talking about "goodness" here: he is affirming the *identity* of
Beauty and Truth, which—like that of Cupid and Psyche—is both
oxymoronic and androgynous, transcending moral categories such
as good and evil.

Indeed the urn, with its four scenes or faces, becomes in Jungian
terms a mandala or symbol of psychic wholeness, like Blake's *Four
Zoas* and T. S. Eliot's *Four Quartets*. According to Elizabeth Drew,
who interpreted the latter, "Jung asserts that the mandala dream
image always combines the elements of circular rotation . . . some
element of fourness, and the all-important center."[20] Keats emphasizes the circular rotation of the urn in the companion "Ode on
Indolence," which is echoed by the moving stillness of the Chinese
jar in Eliot's "Burnt Norton"; but the idea of rotation is also implicit in the more centered "Ode on a Grecian Urn," where the
reader is invited to behold each of the urn's four "faces" in turn.
The urn's ovoid shape also reminds one of Plato's androgyne.
Hence Keats's preference for the sort of happiness offered by the
urn—which he also attributed to the singing nightingale—in lieu
of "All breathing human passion" (28) that leaves one separate
and unsatisfied.

The urn's oxymoronic doubleness replicating to fourfoldness is
symbolically indicated from the beginning of the poem, where
Keats endows the urn, both explicitly and by implication, with two
sets of parents: "silence and slow time," as well as the earthen
material of which the urn in made and its nameless sculptor. This
quaternity reinforces the idea of the "flattened-out" urn (compare
Blake's view of the world as an "infinite plane" [*M*, 15:32]) as a
mandala, which Jung calls "the archetypal image of God as manifested in his creation," citing the visions of Ezekiel and Saint John
the Divine as illustrations. Jung adds, "The central Christian symbol is a Trinity, but the formula of the unconscious mind is a
quaternity."[21]

Keats also, as has been frequently noted, endows the urn with
paradoxical and punning offspring—"brede / Of marble men and
maidens overwrought" (41–42)—with the phrasing again emphasizing gender balance. Finally, the urn as an aspect of Sophia,
Divine Wisdom, becomes a secular Christ figure, "a friend to man"
(48), physically vulnerable but able to articulate the eternal identity

of (feminine) beauty and (masculine) truth through the sublime androgyny of art.

False versus Sublime Androgyny

Lamia, which I have discussed at length elsewhere,[22] is an extended exercise in romantic irony, in which the male and female roles of the typical quest romance are reversed. Accordingly, Keats excoriates the dreamer Lycius, a young student of philosophy *manqué;* the serpent-woman Lamia, his sensual dream; and the sophist Apollonius who, like certain contemporary theorists, can "see through" but not create. When Lycius and Lamia quarrel over his proposal of marriage—to be celebrated by a triumphal procession related symbolically to Corinthian imperialism—Keats indicates that their relationship, far from being ideally androgynous, is based on the old "macho" model of male domination and female mock-submissiveness:

> His passion, cruel grown, took on a hue
> Fierce and sanguineous as 'twas possible
> In one whose brow had no dark veins to swell. . . .
> She burnt, she lov'd the tyranny.
> And, all subdued, consented to the hour
> When to the bridal he should lead his paramour.
>
> (2.75–83)

As one might have expected in a poem of this sort, brilliant though it is, the motif of androgyny is for the most part conspicuous by its absence. Its hermaphroditic counterpart is seen in Keats's portrayal of the predatory Lamia, whose serpentine appearance draws on the old tradition according to which serpent equals phallus: Lycius is, in a sense, being attacked by his own penis.[23] All this symbolizes the death of poetry, as in Coleridge's "Christabel" (which also employs the serpent-woman motif). After Lycius's illusory world has been destroyed, along with his own life, his body is wound in its cocoonlike marriage robe (2.311), completing the motif of false androgyny.

In "To Autumn"—for all practical purposes Keats's last completed poem—he presents a vision of nature revealed in human form. Autumn is fully humanized throughout, beginning with the first stanza, where she (though Keats, like Blake in "To Spring," carefully avoids specifying the Season's gender) is described as "[c]lose bosom-friend of the maturing sun; / Conspiring with him" to fecundate the vines and fruit trees. "Close bosom-friend" suggests a relationship closer to agape than eros, and "conspiring," which means literally "breathing together," implies a creative complicity more androgynous than otherwise. Keats seems to be using the word in the sense of "combining in action or aim," as distinct from the more common legal meaning, although there are hints of something sensuous, pleasurable, and innocently secret in the workings of the *natura naturans,* an impression that is also conveyed by the tactile quality of the words "swell" and "plump."

The second stanza presents Autumn in a variety of pastoral poses. Thus she is portrayed "sitting careless on a granary floor," with her hair "soft-lifted by the winnowing wind"—with the gentle irony that the wind is doing Autumn's work for her—"Or on a half-reap'd furrow sound asleep," while her hook "Spares the next swath and all its twined flowers," as though death itself is held in abeyance. Keats also compares Autumn to "a gleaner," recalling the famous reference to Ruth in the penultimate stanza of "Ode to a Nightingale"; by an extension of the same simile, he portrays her as either a woman crossing a brook with a basket of gleanings on her head, or a humanized fruit tree bending with "laden head across a brook," in either case anticipating (and perhaps influencing) Samuel Palmer's golden harvest scenes, with their sublime sense of rest after labor.

Keats's remark in his letter to Reynolds written two days after this valedictory poem that he "always somehow associate[s] Chatterton with autumn"[24] shows that he was facing the prospect of his own imminent death. Nevertheless, this is the most serene of the odes: in the warm, sensuous, fecundating figure of Autumn Keats found the perfect objective correlative of his own poetical character. Thus the poem leaves one with a sense of completion, of a process having reached its fulfilment. But there is nothing static about this: in Coleridge's phrase referring to the nature of poetic symbolism, Keats is here revealing the "translucence of the eternal through and in the temporal."[25] Thus he becomes what he beholds, a bounteous lover, as androgynous and sublime as Cleopatra's vision of Mark Antony after his death:

> For his bounty
> There was no winter in't; an autumn 'twas
> That grew the more by reaping.
>
> (5.2.86–88)

Conclusion

WE HAVE OBSERVED THAT THE MODE AND MOTIF OF THE AN-
drogynous sublime constitutes a major, hitherto neglected, aspect
of English romantic poetry. We have also seen how this mode
subverts conventional or "phallic" notions of sublimity, confirming
my postulate regarding the androgynous nature of the poetical
character. Further, recent research, much of it influenced by Jungian psychology, has begun to reveal that Plato's fable of an original
androgyne (which has counterparts in the Book of Genesis and
elsewhere in the Bible) is one of the great informing myths of Western culture. Why, then, has it taken so long for this awareness
to emerge?

No doubt there are social as well as cultural reasons, but I would
like to suggest one that may well have been overlooked: Plato's
uncharacteristic use of humor. His portrayal of Aristophanes in the
Symposium, as well as the comedian's narration of a tale involving
humanoid billiard balls, has doubtless had a hermetic effect, ren-
dering the myth a sort of time capsule, if not a time bomb (except
to a few initiates). Shelley, almost alone among the romantics,
seems to have fully appreciated this and responded to it in kind,
in "The Witch of Atlas," with predictable results: even his wife
condemned it (humor was never Mary's strong point), leaving posterity, beginning with Yeats, to relish the jest and savor its
significance.

For some reason we tend to devalue humor, typically dismissing
it as lightweight or "just funny." (Hegel saw humor as a form of
self-transcendence, virtually sublime.) No doubt this attitude is a
carryover from Matthew Arnold's concept of literary "touch-
stones" and the "high seriousness" he considered a necessary attri-
bute of great art. Shakespeare, who made Touchstone a Fool (and
his fool a touchstone) knew better. We are now learning to value
the witty paradoxes of Oscar Wilde (which typically comprehend
an androgynous doubleness) more highly than the patriarchal manner of some of the more "eminent" Victorians. Among the moderns
James Joyce's *Finnegans Wake* is revered (and reviled) for what
Northrop Frye referred to as its "linguistic Niagara,"[1] and it would

seem a fair supposition that the cyclical structure of the book of "doublends jined" has some such androgynous overtones as those we have already observed among the writings of Joyce's romantic forerunners.

A rather different example of the androgynous sublime among the moderns is Conrad's portrayal of the mysterious black woman—no doubt Kurtz's mistress—in *Heart of Darkness:*

> She walked with measured steps, draped in striped and fringed cloths, treading the earth proudly, with a light jingle and flash of barbarous ornaments. She carried her head high; her hair was done in the shape of a helmet; she had brass leggings to the knees, brass wire gauntlets to the elbow, a crimson spot on her tawny cheek . . . she was savage and superb, wildeyed and magnificent; there was something ominous and stately in her deliberate progress. And in the hush that had fallen suddenly upon the whole sorrowful land, the immense wilderness, the colossal body of the fecund and mysterious life seemed to look at her, pensive, as though it had been looking at the image of its own tenebrous and passionate soul.[2]

This powerful passage synthesizes elements of Byron's prophetically androgynous poem "Darkness" with Tennyson's portrayal of Sir Lancelot in "The Lady of Shalott."[3] One may compare Conrad's black woman with Sir Lancelot's "coal-black curls" (103), her hair "done in the shape of a helmet" and crimson beauty spot with his "helmet and helmet feather [which] / Burned like one burning flame together" (93–94), her "brass leggings" with his "brazen greaves" (76), and so on. Conrad draws on other analogues as well, no doubt including Baudelaire (Kurtz is said to be part French) and The Song of Solomon: "Thou art beautiful, O my love, as Tirzah, comely as Jerusalem, terrible as an army with banners" (6:4). ("To experience both fear and desire, the male subject must have to some extent internalized the female object."[4]) The androgyne is now a symbolic warrior—she has clearly helped to subvert the slave-owning Kurtz—fighting for psychic and sexual, as well as social liberation, but retaining her own identity: defiant sexuality is affirmed by the "crimson spot on her tawny cheek."

An important corollary of the present study should by now be evident: psychic androgyny, suitably sublimed, may well be a cultural force for personal, and therefore social, transformation. By refining our psychosexual and poetic sensibilities, which are really the same, we may arrive at the state aspired to, and eventually reached, by Keats's Endymion, who explains to his sister Peona that the search for happiness involves not only psychic death and rebirth but also "fellowship with essence": the androgynous unity of being epitomized by poetry and song.

> Feel we these things?—that moment we have stept
> Into a sort of oneness, and our state
> Is like a floating spirit's. But there are
> Richer entanglements, enthralments far
> More self-destroying, leading by degrees
> To the chief intensity: the crown of these
> Is made of love and friendship, and sits high
> Upon the forehead of humanity.
>
> (1.795–802)

Keats goes on to symbolize the distilled essence of friendship and love as "an orbed drop / Of light" which "hangs by unseen film" (1.806–7), as though connecting the temporal and eternal worlds in an androgynous continuum through a psychic fontanel.

Keats's account of this, as he would have been the first to admit, is lacking in humor; but his controlling image of the "orbed drop" reappears suitably transmogrified in a recent story by the surrealist poet and painter Michael Bullock, entitled "The Invulnerable Ovoid Aura." A subtle blend of satire and prophecy, this "far-out fantasy," according to Bullock's foremost interpreter, critic Jack Stewart,

> is a spoof on the scientific report. . . . The concept of an invulnerable aura is said to be drawn from two Phutatorian philosophers of the Middle Ages, Sartorius Maximus (no doubt, a forerunner of Carlyle's Sartor Resartus) and Phallacius Metronomous. . . . The working hypothesis is that certain people with spiritual and artistic affinities can generate an invulnerable aura by forming a close-knit group. . . . Tests establish the optimum configuration for the group to be six people arranged in pairs in "an ovoid or egg shape."[5]

(One is reminded of seeing such configurations spontaneously forming at cocktail parties.) Not only does the ovoid aura protect group members, it also has the power to heal the wounded who are brought within its orbit. "We suspected," Bullock's surrealist narrator remarks, "that, enclosed within [the aura], we might even be immune to an atomic bomb." The six characters, led by the narrator, go on a mythic quest, searching for a strange magnetic mountain that glows in the dark, "said to be shaped like half an egg, as though the lower half of the egg were buried in the ground."[6] The mountain turns out to consist not of matter but of pulsating energy (confirming a speculation of Goethe's), and is "a microcosm of the world of objects as it appears to consciousness."[7] Bullock's egg-shaped mountain invites comparison not only with Plato's androgynous egg, but also with the Sanskrit symbol of God known to Blake and Coleridge.[8]

Stewart, who refers to "The Invulnerable Ovoid Aura" as one of Bullock's "most brilliant and esoteric fables" (274), points out the Swiftian blend of parody and polemics in this tale with intimations of androgyny, which interestingly enough involves a cast of six male artists and intellectuals rather like the sextet of English romantic poets we have been considering. Bullock, whose readership is international as well as esoteric, observes that surrealist writing—like romantic poetry before it—is "a weapon of liberation under all circumstances . . . [Oppressive] regimes cannot tolerate the free exercise and expression of the Imagination and their fear of it is the most convincing proof of its value."[9] One may conclude that if Shelley were alive today he would probably be a surrealist, quite possibly a writer of science fiction, and that when the fascinated auditors of the inspired poet in Coleridge's "Kubla Khan" exclaim "Weave a circle round him thrice," they are doubtless forming an invulnerable ovoid aura. But Coleridge's deepest desire is that the reader should break into that charmed circle and become transformed, for all art is androgynous, aspiring to sublimity.

Notes

Introduction

1. See Thomas Weiskel, *The Romantic Sublime: Studies in the Structure and Psychology of Transcendence* (Baltimore, Mary.: The Johns Hopkins University Press, 1976), 134–36. Diane Long Hoeveler's *Romantic Androgyny: The Women Within* (University Park: Pennsylvania State University Press, 1990) came to my attention after I had substantially completed this book. More psychologically and less stylistically oriented than the present study, and written from a feminist, Marxist, and deconstructive perspective, it presents an interesting contribution to the debate insofar as it acknowledges "the androgynous unification of masculine and feminine qualities within the romantic male psyche" (xiv). About women writers of the period she is silent. More forthcoming in this regard is William Veeder's *Mary Shelley & Frankenstein: The Fate of Androgyny* (Chicago: University of Chicago Press, 1986).

2. See Dionysus Longinus, *On the Sublime,* trans. William Smith, 3rd ed. (London, 1752), passim; John Baillie, *An Essay on the Sublime* (London: 1747), 2. M. H. Abrams does not list *sublime* or *poetry* in the index of his *A Glossary of Literary Terms,* 5th ed. (Fort Worth, Tex.: Holt, Rinehart & Winston, 1988) though he lists *bathos, pathos,* etc.

3. Neil Hertz, *The End of the Line: Essays on Psychoanalysis and the Sublime* (New York: Columbia University Press, 1985), 4–5; Peter de Bolla, in *The Discourse of the Sublime* (Oxford: Blackwell, 1989) curiously remarks that "Longinus avoids the problem of the 'other' . . . by restricting his description of the sublime transport to . . . the orator's experience of masculinity" (56).

4. Edmund Burke, *A Philosophical Inquiry into the Origin of our Ideas of the Sublime and Beautiful* (London, 1759; rpt. New York: Garland, 1971), passim; William Blake, "Annot. Reynolds" [p. 244], *The Poetry and Prose of William Blake,* ed. David V. Erdman (New York: Doubleday, 1970), 650—subsequently cited as *"E."* All quotations from Blake, unless otherwise noted, follow the text of this edition. Vincent Arthur de Luca, *Words of Eternity: Blake and the Poetics of the Sublime* (Princeton: Princeton University Press, 1991), 5, 27.

5. *Symposium.* In *The Works of Plato,* trans. Benjamin Jowett, ed. Irwin Edman (New York: Modern Library, 1956), 353. Some more recent translations substitute the word "hermaphrodite" for "Androgynous" in this passage, thus blurring an important distinction. See Glossary.

6. Plato, *Symposium,* 355–56. See also Carolyn G. Heilbrun, *Toward a Recognition of Androgyny* (New York: Knopf, 1964), xiii.

7. See Robert Graves, *The Greek Myths,* 2 vols. (New York: Brazillier), 1: 27–28; R. J. Stewart, *The Elements of Creation Myth* (Longmead, Shaftesbury, Dorset: Element Books, 1989), 23.

8. Norman O. Brown, *Life Against Death: The Psychoanalytical Meaning of History* (New York: Vintage Books, 1959), 133.

9. See Sara Friedrischmeyer, *The Androgyne in Early German Romanticism: Friedrich Schlegel, Novalis and the Metaphysics of Love,* Stanford German Studies (Bern: Peter Lang, 1983), 30. The quotation is from Boehme's "Mysterium Magnum," as quoted by Friedrischmeyer.

10. Cf. Margaret L. Bailey, *Milton and Jacob Boehme: A Study in Mysticism in Seventeenth-Century England* (New York: Oxford University Press, 1914), 140, et passim.

11. Weiskel, 120. Cf. my *"Kubla Khan* as Symbol," *Texas Studies in Literature and Language* 14 (1973): 603–30.

12. "Mrs. Alfred Uruguay," in *The Collected Poems of Wallace Stevens* (New York: Knopf, 1967), 250.

13. Weiskel, 132.

14. Weiskel, 135.

15. Preface to *Lyrical Ballads, With a Few Other Poems,* 2nd ed. (London: 1800). Reprinted with introduction and notes by R. L. Brett and A. R. Jones (London: Methuen, 1968), 255.

16. Richard Holmes, *Coleridge: Early Visions* (London: Hoddes & Stoughton, 1989), 230; Coleridge, *Table-Talk* (London, n.d. [1835]), 1 September 1832.

Chapter 1. Blake's Myth of Divine Androgyny

1. See, e.g., Harold Bloom, *Blake's Apocalypse: A Study in Poetic Argument* (New York: Anchor Books, 1965), 3.

2. For this illustration see plate 2 in *William Blake: "Tiriel,"* ed. G. E. Bentley, Jr. (Oxford: Oxford University Press, 1967).

3. Benjamin Heath Malkim, *A Father's Memoirs of his Child* (London, 1806), xxxvii. Cf. Longinus, 41.

4. See p. 14 and Note 4 to introduction.

5. See "The Tyger as Los's Artefact," ch. 8 of my *Divine Analogy: A Study of the Creation Motif in Blake and Coleridge* (Salzburg: Salzburg Studies in English, 1972): orig. pub. in *Blake Studies* 2, no. 1 (July 1970): 5–19.

6. See above, Note 5; cf. "The Little Girl Lost," 41 and "The Little Girl Found," 48.

7. Cf. Blake's ref. to "Curiosity a Virgin ever young" in his early prose fragment, "then she bore Pale desire" (*E,* 437).

8. A "curb" is among other things a hard swelling on the hind leg of a horse *(OED).* These two lines were omitted from two of the fifteen extant copies of *Thel.*

9. *Jerusalem,* in *The Poetry and Prose of William Blake,* ed. David V. Erdman (New York: Doubleday), 32:49—subsequently cited as *"J,"* followed by the plate and line numbers. *Milton* is referred to as *"M.",* and is from the same edition unless otherwise indicated.

10. Morton Paley, *Energy and Imagination: A Study of the Development of Blake's Thought* (Oxford: Oxford University Press, 1970), 69.

11. Letter to Hayley, 23 October 1804 (*E,* 702–3).

12. See G. E. Bentley, Jr., *William Blake: "Vala or The Four Zoas"* (Oxford: Oxford University Press, 1963), 163.

13. In conversation with the author.

14. See G. E. Bentley Jr.'s ed. of *The Four Zoas,* 128 (illustrations).

15. William Blake, *The Complete Writings of William Blake,* ed. Geoffrey

Keynes (London: Nonesuch, 1957), 825—subsequently cited as *"K,"* followed by the page numbers.

16. See my *Poetic Friends: A Study of Literary Relations During the English Romantic Period* (New York: Peter Lang, 1990), 26–32, and the Trianon Press (London, 1967) fascism. ed. of *Milton,* plates 45 and 47.

17. Susan Fox, *Poetic Form in Blake's "Milton"* (Princeton: Princeton University Press, 1976), 17.

18. Morton Paley, *The Continuing City: William Blake's "Jerusalem"* (Oxford: Oxford University Press, 1983), 196.

19. "A Vision of the Last Judgment" (*E,* 548; *J,* 32:28).

20. See my "Albany as Archetype in *King Lear," Modern Language Quarterly* 26 (1965): 257–63.

21. W. H. Auden, "The Virgin and the Dynamo," in *The Dyer's Hand, 20th Century Poetry and Poetics,* ed. Gary Geddes, 3rd ed. (Toronto: Oxford University Press, 1985), 524.

22. Stevenson, *Poetic Friends,* 47.

23. Joshua 2:1–6:17; Rev. 17.

24. Blake, "A Descriptive Catalogue" (*E,* 528); cf. *M,* 32:22. See also my "Interpreting Blake's *Canterbury Pilgrims," Colby Library Quarterly* 13, no. 2 (June 1977): 115–26.

25. S. Foster Damon, *A Blake Dictionary* (Providence, R.I.: Brown University Press, 1965), s.v. "Erin."

26. Margaret Atwood, answering a question while addressing the Vancouver Institute, 1988. Cf. Longinus: "Grandeur requires room" (167).

27. For a full-length study of wordplay in Blake see Nelson Hilton, *Literal Imagination: Blake's Vision of Words* (Berkeley: University of California Press, 1983).

28. Marney Jean McGlaughlin Ward, "Text and Design in Blake's Developing Myth" (Ph.D. diss., University of British Columbia, 1973), 258.

29. Ward, 303, 314 (Notes).

30. For full details see David V. Erdman, ed., *The Illuminated Blake* (New York: Anchor Books, 1974), 307–8, and David V. Erdman, "The Suppressed and Altered Passages in Blake's *Jerusalem," Studies in Bibliography* 17 (1964): 1–54.

31. See David V. Erdman, *Prophet Against Empire: A Poet's Interpretation of the History of his Own Times* (Princeton: Princeton University Press, 1954), 440–44.

32. "A Vision of the Last Judgment" (*E,* 549).

33. See Blake, *Europe a Prophecy,* 10:2 (*E,* 63) and John 3:14.

34. See Louis Crompton, *Byron and Greek Love: Homophobia in 19th Century England* (Berkeley: University of California Press, 1985), 17 et passim; Erdman, *Illuminated Blake,* 342.

35. See p. 23 and "Merlin's Prophecy" (*E,* 464). Blake is of course referring to psychic virginity.

36. Cf. *Jerusalem* 59:7–21, wherein Blake contrasts the "beautiful" Mundane Shell with the "sublime" Universe of Los and Enitharmon—in other words, Golgonooza. The former is contained within the latter, as each of Blake's four states of vision nests within the one(s) higher, like a nest of Chinese boxes. Thus there is no bifurcation, only deepening awareness.

37. Erdman, *Illuminated Blake,* 375.

38. Ibid., 378.

39. Los's compass-tongs double this motif, indicating its importance, with the

hinge of the tongs forming a Greek "omega" (as contrasted to the transliteral form of the letter) inside the larger "O," and the levers an "A" within the larger, flowing ones of the now-humanized serpent-temple. Cf. the latter with "Alph, the sacred river" in Coleridge's "Kubla Khan," and cf. also Vincent Arthur De Luca's discussion of Blake's "iconic sublime," which he distinguishes from Blake's "bardic" mode of sublimity. The former refers to the visual appearance of Blake's engraved script (*Words of Eternity,* 62, 80, et passim).

40. The tip of the lever touching Enitharmon's left foot, when taken together with Los's sandalled left foot in plate 1, recapitulates the apocalyptic moment in *Milton.* Similarly, the nine stars surrounding Enitharmon's figure in plate 100 recapitulate the nine nights of *The Four Zoas.* Clearly, the momentum, if not the center of gravity (levity?) has shifted from Los to Enitharmon, now seen as an aspect of Jerusalem.

2. Wordsworth and the Patriarchal Sublime

1. Quotations from Wordsworth's poetry, unless otherwise noted, follow his *Poetical Works,* ed. Thomas Hutchinson, rev. Ernest De Selincourt (London: Oxford University Press, 1960).

2. In the BBC Television series "Civilisation."

3. Annot. Lavater [407], *K,* 77.

4. Alexander Geddes observed in 1790 that "in the language which Moses spoke, the word rendered *voice* signifies, in general, every kind of sound, and . . . particularly the awful sound of thunder" (review of J. Van Eyck, *Ledige Uuren* [1786–90], in *Analytical Review* 7 [1790]; quoted in Robert N. Essick, *William Blake and the Language of Adam* [Oxford: Oxford University Press, 1989], 105).

5. Burke, 303–5 et passim.

6. Longinus, 41.

7. For the fountain of life see Plotinus, *The Essence of Plotinus: Extracts from the Six Enneads . . . ,* ed. Grace H. Turnbull (New York: Oxford University Press, 1934), 3.8.10; cf. the River of Life in Rev. 22:1–2. Cf. also line 199 of the Immortality Ode with 1 Cor. 9:24.

8. See my "Wordsworth and the Stone of Night," *The Wordsworth Circle* 13, no. 4 (Autumn 1982):175–78, and *The Myth of the Golden Age in English Romantic Poetry,* Romantic Reassessment 109 (Salzburg: Salzburg Studies in English Literature, 1983), 30–31.

9. Weiskel, 198.

10. Ibid., 199.

11. "The whole of the day [23 September 1816] as fine in point of weather as the day on which Paradise was made" (*Byron: A Self-Portrait in His Own Words,* ed. Peter Quenel [Oxford: Oxford University Press, 1990], 353). Byron's "Wengren Mountain," the highest he climbed in the Alps, is now called the Lauberhorn. See John Clubbe and Ernest Giddey, *Byron et la Suisse: deux études* [Geneva: Librairie Droz, 1982], 18–26. Cf. p. 136.

12. See, e.g., the discussion of Wordsworth in my *Nimbus of Glory: A Study of Coleridge's Three Great Poems,* Romantic Reassessment 109, no. 2 (Salzburg: Salzburg Studies in English Literature, 1983), 60–63 et passim; Weiskel, 181–83 et passim.

13. I find Weiskel's suggestion that Wordsworth's "ritual chastisement . . . covers (from himself) a deeper refusal to bow low" (184) particularly interesting.

14. See my "Wordsworth's 'Satanism,'" *The Wordsworth Circle* 15, no. 2 (Sum-

mer 1984), 82–84, Cf. the Lamb, wall, and tree mentioned continguously in Rev. 21:17–23; 22:2.

15. Geoffrey H. Hartman, *Wordsworth's Poetry: 1787–1814* (New Haven: Yale University Press, 1964), in his sensitive discussion of the Mount Snowdon passage, grants it a kind of sublimity (189–90), but also calls it Wordsworth's "greatest avoidance of apocalypse" because of its reliance on Nature (254). As Hartman explains in his preface (x), he uses the term *apocalypse* primarily in the biblical sense, whereas I use it to mean any authentic revelation (see Glossary). Seen in this light, the Mount Snowdon passage, for all its use of what Hartman calls "boundary images," is more apocalyptic than the Gondo Gorge one.

16. Frances Ferguson, *Wordsworth: Language as Counter-Spirit* (New Haven: Yale University Press, 1977), 207.

17. Coleridge called "A slumber did my Spirit seal" "a most sublime Epitaph" (*The Collected Letters of Samuel Taylor Coleridge*, vol. 2, ed. E. L. Griggs (Oxford: Oxford University Press, 1956), 817.

18. Hartman, 162. Hartman's felicitous observation about "the beautifully in-obvious use of the transferred epithet, 'I had no human fears,'" and his reference to "A Slumber . . ." as one of "the most haunting" of Wordsworth's poems (158–59) tend to meliorate his position.

3. Coleridge: From the Analogical to the Androgynous Sublime

1. Samuel Taylor Coleridge, *The Complete Poetical Works of Samuel Taylor Coleridge*, ed. E. H. Coleridge, 2 vols. (Oxford: Oxford University Press, 1912; rpt. 1966), 112–13. Quotations from Coleridge's poetry follow the text of this edition.

2. See my *Divine Analogy*, ch. 7, 10 et passim.

3. Coleridge, *Collected Letters*, 1034.

4. Cf. Raimonda Modiano's observation that for "Coleridge the sublime represents the highest form of unity," transcending both visible objects per se and a sense of personal egotism (*Coleridge and the Concept of Nature* [London: Macmillan, 1985], 122–28).

5. See my "Coleridge's Divine Duplicity: Being a Concatenation of His Surrogates, Succedanemus, and Doppelgangers," *The Wordsworth Circle* 20, no. 2 (1989): 74–78.

6. See my *Nimbus of Glory*, 79ff. Cf. Robert Penn Warren, *The Rime of The Ancient Mariner with an Essay by Robert Penn Warren* (New York: Reynal and Hitchcock, 1949), 86–99.

7. "To Dr Trusler" (*K*, 793); Annot. Reynolds (*K*, 457).

8. Byron's note to "The Siege of Corinth," *The Works of Lord Byron* (Paris, 1828), 202.

9. The following show similarities to "Christabel": Scott in "The Lay of the Last Minstrel" and "The Lady of the Lake," Wordsworth in "The White Doe of Rylestone," and Byron in "The Siege of Corinth" to which he appended a note (see above, note 8) maintaining he had not been "a wilful plagiarist." See my "Byron and Coleridge: The Eagle and the Dove," *The Byron Journal* 19 (1991): 116.

10. For the view that Christabel's ravishment is meant to be physical rather than psychic see "The Daemon as Lesbian Vampire," ch. 12 in Camille Paglia's

lurid, overwritten *Sexual Personae: Art and Decadence from Nefertiti to Emily Dickinson* (New Haven: Yale University Press, 1990).

11. *"Christabel:* a Re-interpretation," in my *Nimbus of Glory,* 3–24; orig. pub. in *Alphabet,* No. 4 (1962): 18–35. For a more succinct statement of the case see my *Poetic Friends,* 93–108.

12. Hazlitt took the bold guess that Geraldine was a man in disguise and challenged Coleridge to reveal his true identity (*The Complete Works of William Hazlitt,* ed. P. P. Howe, vol. 19 [London: J. M. Dent, 1931]), 33.

13. See my *Myth of the Golden Age,* 47–49. Cf. Crashaw's "Hymn to Sainte Teresa," 43–64, *The Complete Poetry of Richard Crashaw,* ed. George Walton Williams (New York: New York University Press, 1972), 55.

14. Unpub. notebook no. 30, 60v.

15. Susan Luther, "A Different Lore: Coleridge's 'The Nightingale,'" *The Wordsworth Circle* 22, no. 2 (1989): 91.

16. Blake, *The Marriage of Heaven and Hell* (*K,* 151).

17. Luther, 94–95.

18. For further discussion of this passage see Tillotama Rajan, *Dark Interpreter: The Discourse of Romanticism,* (Ithaca: Cornell University Press, 1980), 226, and my "Coleridge's Divine Duplicity," 75–76.

19. Plato, *Symposium,* 354.

20. These lines anticipate Teilhard de Chardin's concept of the Noosphere, or envelope of mind surrounding the earth, and are doubly androgynous, working something like a reversible raincoat. See Pierre Teilhard de Chardin, *The Phenomenon of Man* (New York: Harper, 1958), 180–83.

21. But note that Coleridge portrays his "immortal mind" as "God's Image, sister of the Seraphim" in the last line of "Ode to the Departing Year."

22. Francis Thompson, *Selected Poems* (London: Methuen, n.d.), 78–79.

23. Cf. the discussion of "The Tyger," p. 26.

24. One of my students observed that the curious pulsating rhythm of this poem suggests a kind of submerged sexuality.

25. "A Descriptive Catalogue" (*K,* 585).

26. "To a friend who had left Racedown early in 1797," Christopher Wordsworth, *Memoirs of William and Dorothy Wordsworth by Christopher Wordsworth,* ed. Henry Reed (Boston, 1851; rpt. New York: AMS Press, 1966), 1:99. See also "The Symbolic Unity of *Kubla Khan*" in my *Nimbus of Glory,* 25–59, orig. pub. as "*Kubla Khan* as Symbol," *Texas Studies in Literature and Language* 14, no. 4 (1973): 603–30.

27. See Thomas Maurice, *The History of Hindostan,* Vol. 1 (London: 1795–98), 50–67 and plate 2 showing the Mundane Egg of Heliopolis. Cf. the discussion of this in my "*Kubla Khan* as Symbol," 621–23.

28. Rev. 21:6; cf. Rev. 1:8–11, 22–13.

4. Byron's Sublime Androgyny

1. See Crompton, 105 et passim.

2. All quotations from Byron's poetry, unless otherwise noted, follow the text of *Lord Byron. The Complete Poetical Works,* ed. Jerome J. McGann, 5 vols. (Oxford: Oxford University Press, 1980–86).

3. Stevenson, *Myth of the Golden Age,* ch. 4.

4. In a public lecture given at the University of British Columbia, 1969.

5. Cf. p. 14.

6. *Threefold Life*, xi.12.; v.44 and *Forty Questions Concerning the Soul,* no. 1.116, both in *The Works of Jacob Behmen, The Teutonic Philosopher* [Ed. George Ward and William Langcake, with . . . notes and interpolations by William Law], 4 vols (London, 1764–81). Subsequent quotations from Boehme follow this edition unless otherwise noted.

7. Cf. *Byron: A Self-Portrait*, 352, where Byron refers to an inscription commemorating a similar incident in the area.

8. Ibid., 323. For the spelling of "Wengren" see Clubbe and Giddey, 24.

9. See Malcom Elwin, *Lord Byron's Wife* (London: Macdonald, 1962), 263.

10. Cf. Donald H. Reiman's remark that Juan combines "personal physical courage . . . with his tenderness as a lover and as the protector of helpless innocents" ("*Don Juan* in Epic Context," *Studies in Romanticism* 16, no. 4 (Fall 1977): 593).

11. Plato, *Symposium*, 357.

12. See Leslie A. Marchand, ed. *Don Juan* (Boston: Riverside, 1958), 470 (notes).

13. Susan J. Wolfson, "'Their She Condition': Cross-Dressing and the Politics of Gender in *Don Juan*," *English Literary History* 54 (1987): 585–617.

14. Jacques Derrida, "La Loi du Genre/The Law of Genre," tr. Avitall Ronell, *Glyph Textual Studies 7,* 203–4; quoted by Wolfson, 593.

15. Wolfson, 601.

16. Cf. Harold Bloom's remark that "irony . . . destroys the Sublime" (introduction, *Poets of Sensibility and the Sublime* [New York: Chelsea House, 1986], 6). Byron's growing awareness of this truth, reflected in the fact that canto 2 of *Don Juan* is both the most sublime and the least ironic of the cantos, may also help to explain his deliberate turning away from irony in his last completed long poem, *The Island.* See my *Poetic Friends,* 164–67 and "Hebraism and Hellenism in the Poetry of Byron," in *Byron, The Bible, and Religion: Essays from the Twelfth International Byron Seminar,* ed. Wolf Hirst (Newark: University of Delaware Press, 1991), 136–52.

5. Shelley's Androgynous Quest

1. Thomas Jefferson Hogg, *Shelley at Oxford;* quoted by Francis Berry, *Poetry and the Physical Voice* (London: Routledge, 1962), 67.

2. Francis Thompson, *Shelley,* 9th ed. (London: Burns, Oates & Washbourne, 1925), 27.

3. See Richard Holmes, *Shelley: The Pursuit* (London: Weidenfield and Nicolson, 1974), 40, 90, 214–15, 275–77.

4. Quotations from Shelley's poetry unless otherwise noted follow the text of *The Complete Poetical Works of Percy Bysshe Shelley,* ed. Thomas Hutchinson (London: Oxford University Press, 1905; rpt. 1960). Quotations from his prose follow the text of *The Complete Works of Percy Bysshe Shelley,* ed. Roger Ingpen and Walter E. Peck 10 vols. (New York: Gordian, 1965).

5. Desmond King-Hele, *Shelley: His Thought and Work,* 2nd ed. (London: Macmillan, 1971), 88.

6. To Maria Gisborne, 16 November 1819, in Shelley, *Complete Works,* 10 (*Letters*) no. 442, p. 124.

7. See Rev. 1:14–18; 12: 1–5. Cf. Ezek. ch. 1.

8. See my *Myth of the Golden Age,* 86–87.

9. Quotations from "Song of Apollo" and "Song of Pan" follow the text of

Shelley's Poetry and Prose, ed. Donald H. Reiman and Sharon B. Powers (New York: Norton, 1977).

10. Cf. the ironic force of "rocked" in relation to "cradle" ("Its passions will rock thee") (24–25) in "Lines: 'When the Lamp is Shattered,'" the most poignant of Shelley's poems.

11. For a photo of this statue see Holmes, *Shelley,* Fig. 29.

12. Ibid., 607.

13. Shelley, *Complete Works,* 7.183; emphasis added. Cf. Jowett's trans. of this passage given p. 15, and Note. Shelley has minimized the "reproach."

14. Jerrold E. Hogle, "Metaphor and Metamorphosis in Shelley's 'The Witch of Atlas,'" *Studies in Romanticism* 19 (Fall 1980): 328.

15. For a more complete discussion of Yeatsian parallels with this poem see Harold Bloom, who in *The Visionary Company: A Reading of English Romantic Poetry* (New York: Anchor Books, 1963), (349–52) observes that *"The Witch of Atlas* seems to have haunted the imagination of the old Yeats."

16. Shelley, *Complete Works* 10 *(Letters)* no. 526, p. 270; no. 529, p. 275; Keats, *The Letters of John Keats,* ed. M. Buxton Forman, 3rd ed. (Oxford: Oxford University Press, 1948), No. 227, p. 507.

17. Ross Greig Woodman, *The Apocalyptic Vision in the Poetry of Shelley* (Toronto: University of Toronto Press, 1964), xiii.

6. Keats's Immortal Androgyny

1. William Hazlitt, *Table-Talk, Or, Original Essays* (London, 1821–22) in *The Complete Works of William Hazlitt,* ed. P. P. Howe (London, J. M. Dent, 1931), 8:253–55.

2. Quoted from my "Mary Coleridge," in *Modern British Essayists,* vol. 98, *Dictionary of Literary Biography,* 1st series, (Detroit: Gale Research, 1990), 76.

3. John Keats, *The Letters of John Keats,* ed. Hyder E. Rollins, 2 vols. (Cambridge: Harvard University Press, 1958), 2:67; 1:386–77.

4. Byron, as quoted in Thomas Medwin, *Medwin's Conversations of Lord Byron,* ed. E. J. Lovell, Jr. (Princeton: Princeton University Press, 1966), 165; Northrop Frye, "Lord Byron," in *Fables of Identity: Studies in Poetic Mythology* (New York: Harcourt, Brace, 1963), 184. Cf. Note 10 to ch. 4, above.

5. See Walter Jackson Bate, *John Keats* (New York: Oxford University Press, 1966), 86ff.

6. Wolfson, 602–3.

7. Keats, *Letters,* ed. Rollins, 1: 193–94.

8. Quotations from Keats's poetry follow the text of *The Poetical Works of John Keats,* ed. H. Buxton Forman (Oxford: Oxford University Press, 1906).

9. See my *Myth of the Golden Age,* 96–99.

10. To J. H. Reynolds, 21 September 1819 (Keats, *Letters,* ed. Rollins, 2:116).

11. Morris Dickstein, *Keats and His Poetry: A Study in Development* (Chicago: University of Chicago Press, 1971), 186.

12. Dickstein, 190.

13. Dickstein, 190.

14. Keats, "On the Grasshopper and the Cricket," *Poetical Works,* 41.

15. To Tom Keats, 9 July 1818 (Keats, Letters, ed. Rollins, 2:320). Cf. "buried deep," 1. 77.

16. Cf. my *Myth of the Golden Age,* 101.

17. Cf. p. 90 and ch. 4, Note 6.

18. Marjorie Garson's highly politicized interpretation of this poem—"Bodily Harm: Keats's Figures in 'Ode on a Grecian Urn,'" *English Studies in Canada* 26, no. 1 (March 1991): 37–51—is too complex to be fully answered in a brief note, but its scenario of a "gang rape" taking place in st. 1 not only fails to account satisfactorily for the "pipes and timbrels" mentioned in the same stanza, but also ignores the related point that the ritual pursuit of the bride(s) was, and still is in certain parts of the world, an integral part of primitive marriage ceremonies, such as the one described in Joyce Cary's novel *Mister Johnson* (London: Penguin Books, 1962).

19. See *The Teaching of Buddha* (Tokyo: Bukko Dendo Kyokai, 1986), passim.

20. Elizabeth Drew, *T. S. Eliot: The Design of His Poetry* (New York: Scribner's, 1949), 142.

21. Carl Jung, *Two Essays on Analytical Psychology* 265; quoted by Drew, 143.

22. Warren Stevenson, "*Lamia:* A Stab at the Gordian Knot," *Studies in Romanticism* 2, no. 3 (Summer 1972): 241–52.

23. For an instructive analogue see Blake's illustration to his poem "To the Accuser who is The God of This World," where a bat-winged Lucifer emerges from the snaky, semierect penis of a recumbent dreamer. Above, a serpent with ten numbered coils recapitulates the motif of false androgyny (Erdman, *Illuminated Blake*, 279). Cf. also Keats's cryptic reference in *Lamia* (1.390) to "a few Persian mutes" as symbolic counterparts to Lamia and Lycius.

24. Keats, *Letters,* ed. Rollins, 2: 167.

25. From *The Stateman's Manual,* in *The Portable Coleridge,* ed. I. A. Richards (New York: Viking, 1950), 388.

Conclusion

1. Northrop Frye, "Cycle and Apocalypse in *Finnegans Wake,*" in *Vico and Joyce,* ed. Donald Phillip Verene (Albany: State University Press of New York, 1987), 7.

2. Joseph Conrad, *Heart of Darkness,* ed. Robert Kimbrough (New York: Norton, 1971), 61–62.

3. Alfred Tennyson, *Tennyson's Poetry: Authoritative Texts,* ed. Robert W. Hill, Jr. (New York: Norton, 1971).

4. Morton Paley, letter to the author, 5 July 1992. Cf. Milton, *Paradise Lost,* 9: 489–91.

5. Jack Stewart, *The Incandescent Word: The Poetic Vision of Michael Bullock* (London, Ont.: Third Eye, 1990), 271–72.

6. Michael Bullock, *The Invulnerable Ovid Aura and Other Stories* (London, Ont.: Third Eye), 13–17.

7. Jack Stewart, 273; cf. Jack Stewart, 307, Note 1.

8. See p. 84 and Blake's "Mundane Shell," *M,* 19:15 (*K,* 500), passim. In another of Bullock's fictions, *Randolph Cranstone and the Pursuing River,* the protagonist "metamorphoses into Randolpha . . . [whereupon] Randolph and Randolpha coexist as brother/sister before the split self is reunified" (Jack Stewart, 119). The motif of the androgyne continues to bulk large in Bullock's writings, although he professes his ignorance of Plato's *Symposium.* Compare the protagonist's vision of a glowing, godlike egg in ch. 19 of Margaret Atwood's *The Handmaid's Tale* (Toronto: McClelland and Stewart, 1985). Cf. also Heather Spears's (twin) novels *Moonfall* (Victoria, B.C.: Beach Holme, Tesseract Books, 1991) and *The Children of Atwar* (Victoria, B.C.: Beach Holme, Tesseract Books, 1993), set

in a postholocaust world inhabited by bicephalic human twins sharing the same body, whose unicephalic savior is also a victim. It is perhaps worth noting that Spears, like Bullock, is also a poet and visual artist.

9. Michael Bullock, "Some Thoughts on Writing," quoted by Stewart, 302, Note 3. In Germany to this day androgynous given names are forbidden by the state.

Glossary

Analogical Sublime: Used with reference to certain passages in Coleridge's early poetry and prose that develop "the divine analogue," or symbolic relation between human and divine creativity.

Androgyne: A being that combines characteristics of both sexes. As used in this study the word pertains primarily to psychic or imaginative androgyny.

Androgynous sublime: That mode of sublimity which, characterized by a limber style suffused with intimations of androgyny, stands in marked contrast to Edmund's Burke's "terrible sublime," Wordsworth's egotistical or patriarchal sublime, and Weiskel's "phallic sublime," although any combination of these may coexist within a given work.

Androgyny: Imaginative union of the two sexes, as in Blake's formulation: "The Sexual is Threefold: the Human is Fourfold" (*M*, 2:5). Cf.: "The Imagination is not a State: it is the Human Existence itself" (*M*, 32:32).

Apocalyptic: As used herein, pertaining to any authentic mode of revelation. The locus classicus is of course The Revelation of Saint John the Divine.

Liminal: Approaching the threshold; at or near the boundary between the mundane and the sublime.

Negative sublime: A mode of sublimity attained, or aspired to, through irony or indirection, as in certain parts of *Don Juan.*

Sublime: Traditionally, elevated or transcendent in style, but in the androgynous mode often paradoxically welling up from below. The word, with its complicated etymology (see pp. 14–15), is itself an oxymoron, which helps to give it undertones of androgyny.

Works Cited

Abrams, M. H. *A Glossary of Literary Terms.* 5th ed. Fort Worth, Tex.: Holt, Rinehart & Winston, 1988.

Atwood, Margaret. *The Handmaid's Tale.* Toronto: McClelland and Stewart, 1985.

Auden, W. H. "The Virgin and the Dynamo." In *The Dyer's Hand, 20th Century Poetry and Poetics,* edited by Gary Geddes, 520–25. 3rd ed. Toronto: Oxford University Press, 1985.

Bailey, Margaret L. *Milton and Jacob Boehme: A Study in Mysticism in Seventeenth-Century England.* New York: Oxford University Press, 1914.

Baillie, John. *On the Sublime.* London, 1747.

Bate, Walter Jackson. *John Keats.* New York: Oxford University Press, Galaxy Books, 1966.

Bentley, G. E., Jr. *William Blake: "Vala or The Four Zoas."* Oxford: Oxford University Press, 1963.

Berry, Francis, *Poetry and the Physical Voice.* London: Routledge, 1962.

Blake, William. *The Complete Writings of William Blake.* Edited by Geoffrey Keynes. London: Nonesuch, 1957.

———. *Milton a Poem.* [1804–1808] Trianon Press facsim. for the William Blake Trust. London, 1967.

———. *The Poetry and Prose of William Blake.* Edited by David V. Erdman. New York: Doubleday, 1970.

———. *William Blake: "Tiriel."* Edited by G. E. Bentley, Jr. Oxford: Oxford University Press, 1967.

Bloom, Harold. *Blake's Apocalypse: A Study in Poetic Argument.* New York: Anchor Books, 1965.

———, ed. *Poets of Sensibility and the Sublime.* New York: Chelsea House, 1986.

———. *The Visionary Company: A Reading of English Romantic Poetry.* New York: Anchor Books, 1963.

Boehme Jacob. *The Works of Jacob Behmen, The Teutonic Philosopher.* [Edited by George Ward and Thomas Langcake, with . . . notes and interpolations by William Law.] 4 vols. London, 1764–81.

Brown, Norman O. *Life Against Death: The Psychoanalytical Meaning of History.* New York: Vintage Books, 1959.

Bruce, James. *Travels to Discover the Source of the Nile.* Vol. I, London, 1790–1. 2 vols.

Bullock, Michael. *The Invulnerable Ovoid Aura and Other Stories.* London, Ont.: Third Eye, 1992.

———. *Randolph Cranstone and the Pursuing River.* Vancouver: Rainbird Press, 1975.

Burke, Edmund. *A Philosophical Inquiry into the Origin of our Ideas on the Sublime and Beautiful.* London, 1759: rpt. New York, Garland, 1971.

Byron, George Gordon. *Byron: A Self-Portrait in His Own Words.* Edited by Peter Quennell. Oxford: Oxford University Press, 1990.

———. *Lord Byron: The Complete Poetical Works.* Edited by Jerome J. McGann. 5 vols. Oxford: Oxford University Press, 1980–86.

———. *The Works of Lord Byron.* Paris, 1828.

Cary, Joyce. *Mister Johnson.* London: Penguin Books, 1962.

Chardin, Teilhard de. *The Phenomenon of Man.* New York: Harper, 1958.

Clubbe, John, and Ernest Giddey. *Byron et la Suisse: deux études.* Geneva: Librairie Droz, 1982.

Coleridge, Samuel Taylor. *The Collected Letters of Samuel Taylor Coleridge.* Vol. 2. Edited by E. L. Griggs. Oxford: Oxford University Press, 1956.

———. *The Complete Poetical Works of Samuel Taylor Coleridge.* Edited by E. H. Coleridge. 2 vols. Oxford: Oxford University Press, 1912; rpt. 1966.

———. *The Stateman's Manual.* In *The Portable Coleridge.* Edited by I. A. Richards, 386–94. New York: Viking, 1950.

———. *Table-Talk.* London, n.d. [1835].

Conrad, Joseph. *Heart of Darkness.* Ed. Robert Kimbrough. New York: Norton, 1971.

Crompton, Louis. *Byron and Greek Love: Homophobia in 19th-Century England.* Berkeley: University of California Press, 1985.

Damon, S. Foster. *A Blake Dictionary.* Providence, R.I.: Brown University Press, 1965.

De Bolla, Peter. *The Discourse of the Sublime: Readings in History, Aesthetics, and the Subject.* Oxford: Blackwell, 1989.

De Luca, Vincent Arthur. *Words of Eternity: Blake and the Poetics of the Sublime.* Princeton: Princeton University Press, 1991.

Dickstein, Morris. *Keats and His Poetry: A Study in Development.* Chicago: University of Chicago Press, 1971.

Drew, Elizabeth. *T. S. Eliot: The Design of His Poetry.* New York: Scribner's, 1949.

Elwin, Malcolm. *Lord Byron's Wife.* London: Macdonald, 1962.

Erdman, David V., ed. *The Illuminated Blake.* New York: Anchor Books, 1974.

———. *Prophet Against Empire: A Poet's Interpretation of the History of his Own Times.* Princeton: Princeton University Press, 1954.

———. "The Suppressed and Altered Passages in Blake's *Jerusalem.*" *Studies in Bibliography* 17 (1964): 1–54.

Essick, Robert N. *William Blake and the Language of Adam.* Oxford: Oxford University Press, 1989.

Ferguson, Frances. *Solitude and the Sublime: Romanticism and the Aesthetics of Individuation.* London: Routledge, 1992.

———. *Wordsworth: Language as Counter-Spirit.* New Haven: Yale University Press, 1977.

Fox, Susan. *Poetic Form in Blake's "Milton."* Princeton: Princeton University Press, 1976.

Friedrischmeyer, Sara. *The Androgyne in Early German Romanticism: Friedrich Schlegel, Novalis and the Metaphysics of Love.* Stanford German Studies. Bern: Peter Lang, 1983.

Frye, Northrop. "Cycle and Apocalypse in *Finnegans Wake.*" In *Vico and Joyce,* edited by Donald Phillip Verene, 2–19. Albany: State University of New York Press, 1987.

———. "Lord Byron." In *Fables of Identity: Studies in Poetic Mythology,* 168–89. New York: Harcourt, Brace, 1963.

Garson, Marjorie. "Bodily Harm: Keats's Figures in 'Ode on a Grecian Urn.'" *English Studies in Canada* 26, no. 1 (March 1991): 37–51.

Graves, Robert. *The Greek Myths.* 2 vols. New York: Brazillier. 1957.

Hartman, Geoffrey H. *Wordsworth's Poetry: 1787–1814.* New Haven: Yale University Press, 1964.

Hazlitt, William. *Table-Talk, Or, Original Essays,* in vol. 8 of *The Complete Works of William Hazlitt.* Edited by P. P. Howe. 21 vols. London: J. M. Dent, 1931.

Heilbrun, Carolyn G. *Toward a Recognition of Androgyny.* New York: Knopf, 1964.

Hertz, Neil. *The End of the Line: Essays on Psychoanalysis and the Sublime.* New York: Columbia University Press, 1985.

Hilton, Nelson. *Literal Imagination: Blake's Vision of Words.* Berkeley: University of California Press, 1983.

Hoeveler, Diane Long. *Romantic Androgyny: The Women Within.* University Park: Pennsylvania State University Press, 1990.

Hogle, Jerrold E. "Metaphor and Metamorphosis in Shelley's 'The Witch of Atlas.'" *Studies in Romanticism* 19 (Fall 1980): 320–35.

Holmes, Richard. *Coleridge: Early Visions.* London: Hoddes & Stoughton, 1989.

———. *Shelley: The Pursuit.* London: Weidenfield and Nicolson, 1974.

Kant, Immanuel. *Kant's Critique of Aesthetic Judgment.* Translated by James Creed Meredith. Oxford: Clarendon Press, 1911.

Keats, John. *The Letters of John Keats.* Edited by M. Buxton Forman. 3rd ed. Oxford: Oxford University Press, 1948.

———. *The Letters of John Keats.* Edited by Hyder E. Rollins. 2 vols. Cambridge: Harvard University Press, 1958.

———. *The Poetical Works of John Keats.* Edited by H. Buxton Forman. Oxford: Oxford University Press, 1906.

King-Hele, Desmond. *Shelley: His Thought and Work.* 2nd ed. London: Macmillan, 1971.

Longinus, Dionysius. *On the Sublime.* Translated by William Smith. 3rd ed. London, 1752.

Luther, Susan. "A Different Lore: Coleridge's 'The Nightingale.'" *The Wordsworth Circle* 22, no. 2 (1989): 91–97.

Malkin, Benjamin Heath. *A Father's Memoirs of his Child.* London, 1806.

Marchand, Leslie A., ed. *Don Juan.* Boston: Riverside, 1958.

Maurice, Thomas. *The History of Hindostan.* 2 vols. London, 1795–98.

Medwin, Thomas. *Medwin's Conversations of Lord Byron*. Edited by E. J. Lovell, Jr. Princeton: Princeton University Press, 1966.

Modiano, Raimonda. *Coleridge and the Concept of Nature*. London: Macmillan, 1985.

Paglia, Camille. *Sexual Personae: Art and Decadence from Nefertiti to Emily Dickinson*. New Haven: Yale University Press, 1990.

Paley, Morton. *The Continuing City: William Blake's "Jerusalem."* Oxford: Oxford University Press, 1983.

————. *Energy and Imagination: A Study of the Development of Blake's Thought*. Oxford: Oxford University Press, 1970.

Plato. *Symposium*. In *The Works of Plato*. Translated Benjamin Jowett. Edited Irwin Edman, 333–93. New York: Modern Library, 1956. 333–93.

Plotinus. *The Essence of Plotinus: Extracts from the Six Enneads and Porphyry's Life of Plotinus Based on the Translation by Stephen Mackenna*. Edited by Grace H. Turnbull. New York: Oxford University Press, 1934.

Rajan, Tillotama. *Dark Interpreter: The Discourse of Romanticism*. Ithaca: Cornell University Press, 1980.

Reiman, Donald H. *"Don Juan* in Epic Context." *Studies in Romanticism,* 16, no. 4 (Fall 1977): 587–94.

Shelley, Percy Bysshe. *The Complete Poetical Works of Percy Bysshe Shelley*. Edited by Thomas Hutchinson. London: Oxford University Press, 1905; rpt. 1960.

————. *The Complete Works of Percy Bysshe Shelley*. Edited by Roger Ingpen and Walter E. Peck. 10 vols. New York: Gordian, 1965.

————. *Shelley's Poetry and Prose*. Edited by Donald H. Reiman and Sharon B. Powers. New York: Norton, 1977.

Spears, Heather. *The Children of Atwar*. Victoria, B.C.: Beach Holme, Tesseract Books, 1993.

————. *Moonfall*. Victoria, B.C.: Beach Holme, Tesseract Books, 1991.

Stevens, Wallace. *The Collected Poems of Wallace Stevens*. New York: Knopf, 1967.

Stevenson, Warren. "Albany as Archetype in *King Lear.*" *Modern Language Quarterly* 26 (1965): 257–63.

————. "Byron and Coleridge: The Eagle and the Dove." *The Byron Journal* 19 (1991): 114–27.

————. "Coleridge's Divine Duplicity: Being a Concatenation of His Surrogates, Succedaneums, and Doppelgängers." *The Wordsworth Circle* 20, no. 2 (1989): 74–78.

————. "Hebraism and Hellenism in the Poetry of Byron." In *Byron, the Bible, and Religion: Essays from the Twelfth International Byron Seminar,* edited by Wolf Hirst, 136–52. Newark: University of Delaware Press, 1991.

————. "Interpreting Blake's *Canterbury Pilgrims.*" *Colby Library Quarterly* 13, no. 2 (June 1977): 115–26.

————. *"Kubla Khan* as Symbol." *Texas Studies in Literature and Language* 14 (1973): 603–30.

————. *"Lamia:* A Stab at the Gordian Knot." *Studies in Romanticism* 2, no. 3 (Summer 1972): 241–52.

————. "Mary Coleridge." *In Modern British Essayists.* Vol. 98, *Dictionary of Literary Biography,* 73–76. 1st series. Detroit: Gale Research, 1990.

————. *The Myth of the Golden Age in English Romantic Poetry.* Romantic Reassessment 109. Salzburg: Salzburg Studies in English Literature, 1981.

————. *Nimbus of Glory: A Study of Coleridge's Three Great Poems.* Romantic Reassessment 109, no. 2. Salzburg: Salzburg Studies in English Literature, 1983.

————. *Poetic Friends: A Study of Literary Relations During the English Romantic Period.* New York: Peter Lang, 1990.

————. "Wordsworth and the Stone of Night." *The Wordsworth Circle* 13, no. 4 (Autumn 1982): 175–78.

————. "Wordsworth's 'Satanism.'" *The Wordsworth Circle* 15, no. 2 (Summer 1984): 82–84.

Stewart, Jack. *The Incandescent Word: The Poetic Vision of Michael Bullock.* London, Ont.: Third Eye, 1990.

Stewart, R. J. *The Elements of Creation Myth.* Longmead, Shaftesbury, Dorset: Element Books, 1989.

The Teaching of Buddha. Tokyo: Bukko Dendo Kyokai, 1986.

Teilhard de Chardin, Pierre. *The Phenomenon of Man.* New York: Harper, 1959.

Tennyson, Alfred. *Tennyson's Poetry: Authoritative Texts.* Edited by Robert W. Hill, Jr. New York: Norton, 1971.

Thompson, Francis. *Selected Poems.* London: Methuen, n.d. [c. 1907].

————. *Shelley.* 9th ed. London: Burns Oates & Washbourne, 1925.

Veeder, William. *Mary Shelley and Frankenstein: The Fate of Androgyny.* Chicago: University of Chicago Press, 1986.

Ward, Marney Jean McGlaughlin. "Text and Design in Blake's Developing Myth." Ph.D. Dissertation, University of British Columbia, 1973.

Warren, Robert Penn. *The Rime of the Ancient Mariner with an Essay by Robert Penn Warren.* New York: Reynal and Hitchcock, 1949.

Weiskel, Thomas. *The Romantic Sublime: Studies in the Structure and Psychology of Transcendence.* Baltimore, Mary.: The Johns Hopkins University Press, 1976.

Wolfson, Susan J. "'Their She Condition': Cross-Dressing and the Politics of Gender in *Don Juan.*" *English Literary History* 54 (1987): 585–617.

Woodman, Ross Greig. *The Apocalyptic Vision in the Poetry of Shelley.* Toronto: University of Toronto Press, 1964.

Wordsworth, Christopher. *Memoirs of William and Dorothy Wordsworth by Christopher Wordsworth.* Edited by Henry Reed. Boston, 1851. Rpt. New York: AMS Press, 1966.

Wordsworth, William. *The Poetical Works of Wordsworth.* Edited by Thomas Hutchinson; revised by Ernest De Selincourt. London: Oxford University Press, 1960.

————. Preface to *Lyrical Ballads, With a Few Other Poems.* 2nd ed. London, 1800. Rpt. with Intro. and notes, edited by R. L. Brett and A. R. Jones, 1963. Rpt. London: Methuen, 1968.

Index

Works cited will be found under the author's name.

149

Eve, 16, 30, 59
Ezekiel, 105, 126

Felpham, Sussex, 34
Ferguson, Frances: *Solitude and the Sublime: Romanticism and the Aesthetics of Individuation,* 14
forgiveness, doctrine of: in Blake's myth, 35, 38; in Byron's *Cain,* 87
Fox, Susan, 33–34
France, 41–42, 44, 49, 52–53, 68, 86
French Revolution, 25, 49–50, 58, 68
Freud, Sigmund: psychology of, 17, 18, 60–61; *Beyond the Pleasure Principle,* 15
Frye, Northrop, 13, 81, 116, 129; *Fearful Symmetry,* 17

Galatians, 112
Galway, 42
Genesis, 16, 30, 41, 54–55, 69, 92, 94, 129
George the Third, King, 29
Gibraltar, 42
God: evolving androgynous concept of, 16–17; in Blake, 23–24, 26, 30–31, 44–48; in Wordsworth, 50–51, 53–54, 57, 59, 60–62, 64; in Coleridge, 68, 70, 72, 81, 84; in Byron, 86–87, 90; in Shelley, 101; in Keats, 125–26. *See also* Jesus; Jehovah
Godwin, William: *Political Justice,* 102
Goethe, Johann Wolfgang von, 132
Golden Age, 17, 84, 87, 93, 96, 103, 110–11
Gondo Gorge, 58
Gray, Thomas: "The Bard," 17

Hartman, Geoffrey, 65
Hayley, William, 33
Hazlitt, William: "On Effeminacy of Character," 116–17; 138
Hegel, Georg Wilhelm Friedrich, 129
hermaphrodite, 41, 45, 86, 109, 127
Hobhouse, John, 60
homosexuality, 15, 34, 42, 76, 86, 112
Heracleitus, 14
Hermes, 57, 110
Hertz, Neil: *The End of the Line,* 13
Hogg, Thomas Jefferson, 101–2
Holy Spirit, the, 16

Homer, 117–18; *The Odyssey,* 96
Hunt, Leigh, 118
Hutchinson, Sara, 80
Hyacinthus, 106–7

imagination, 33, 35, 56, 65, 69, 73, 76–77; and androgyny, 34–36, 41–42, 46–48, 65, 73–77, 80–81, 84–85, 124
incest, 89, 93; and androgyny, 103, 107
Ireland, 37, 41
Israelites, 85

Jacob, 44
Jehovah, 46; in Bible, 85; Blake's portrayal of, 42, 46; in Byron's *Cain,* 87
Jesus, 17; Blake's portrayal of, 23, 27, 30–31, 35–36, 42, 46; and Wordsworth, 52, 54, 59; and Coleridge, 84; and Shelley, 105, 112, 115; and Keats, 125–26
John the Divine, Saint, 54, 59, 84, 126. *See also* Revelation
Jones, Robert, 58–60
Joseph, 42
Joyce, James: *Ulysses,* 42, 95; *Finnegans Wake,* 37, 110, 129–30
Joyce, Nora, 42
Jung, Carl: psychology of, 15, 65, 126, 162
Jungfrau, 93

Kabbala, 29
Kant, Immanuel: *Critique of Aesthetic Judgment,* 29
Kean, Edmund, 80
Keats, John, 15, 65, 78, 113–15; androgyous poetical character of, 116; theory of negative capability related to androgyny, 117; and Plato's myth of androgyne, 120, 126; *Endymion,* 116, 119, 121, 130–31; *Hyperion,* 116, 121–23; "Lamia," 116, 123, 127; "Isabella, or the Pot of Basil," 116, 120; "On First Looking Into Chapman's Homer," 117; "To Homer," 117–19; "I Stood Tip-Top," 118; "Sleep and Poetry," 118–19; "After Dark Vapours," 119; "On the Sea," 119; "The Eve of St. Agnes," 120–21, 123; "To Autumn," 123, 127–28; "Ode to Psyche," 123–24; "Ode to a Nightin-